more
peas,
thank you

more
peas,
thank you

Over 85 Vegetarian Recipes
for Delicious and Healthy Meals

New York Times Bestselling Author
Sarah Matheny

More Peas, Thank You
ISBN-13: 978-0-373-89272-3
© 2013 by Sarah Matheny

Library of Congress Cataloging-in-Publication Data
Matheny, Sarah.
    More peas, thank you : 85+ vegetarian recipes for delicious and
    healthy meals / Sarah Matheny.
        pages cm.
        Includes index.
    ISBN 978-0-373-89272-3
    1. Vegetarian cooking. 2. Cooking, American. 3. Cookbooks. I. Title.
    TX837.M3943 2012
    641.5'636—dc23
    2012017081

Photography by Ashley McLaughlin on pages xiv (Pea Daddy and Gigi photos), xv (Lulu photo), 42, 47, 82, 89, 92, 95, 98, 135, 148, 170, 172, 175, 178, 211, 223, 225, 233.

Photography by Megan M. Jones on pages xiii and xiv (Mama Pea photo).

www.Harlequin.com

Printed in U.S.A.

For the readers of *Peas and Thank You*.
For bloggers, mommies, foodies, family and friends.
Your comments make me smile.
Your encouragement sparks my creativity.
Your support forever changed my five-year plan.
I am grateful for you every single day.
You want More Peas? You got it. It's the least I can do.

acknowledgments

I ACKNOWLEDGE THAT WITHOUT MY SAVIOR, I CAN DO NOTHING (JOHN 15:5) BUT WITH HIM, ALL THINGS ARE POSSIBLE (MATTHEW 19:26).

I acknowledge that I have the world's greatest kids. You, sweet girls, have given me a few well-earned gray hairs, but far more smile lines and belly laughs. Thanks for being my sous chefs, my taste-testers and my motivation for just about everything I do. May you always know how loved you are. Just. For. Being.

I acknowledge the selfless help of my parents; my family and my dear friends; my agent, Lisa Grubka, and editor, Sarah Pelz, in bringing this book into being. Thank you.

I acknowledge that Ashley McLaughlin is a far finer photographer than I could ever hope to be. I feel so grateful to have you again be a part of our book and even more grateful for your friendship.

I acknowledge that behind this try-hard, strong-willed and imperfect woman is a patient, kind and loving man. Chris, you may have had no idea what you signed up for almost ten years ago, but man, did I hit the jackpot. Cha-ching.

I acknowledge that this life is delicious. May you always laugh with your mouth full.

contents

Introduction   xi
Meet the Peas   xiii
In the Peas' Pantry   xvii

48 Snacks, Sides and Sauces

100 Soups, Salads and Sandwiches

Breakfasts **xxiv**

Dinners 136

184 Desserts

Menu Planning	238
Converting to Metrics	240
Index	241
About the Author	248

introduction

WE ARE NOT YOUR NORMAL FAMILY. AND YET WE ARE.

Sure, I cook dinner at 9:00 a.m. so I can photograph it in the best possible light and show it to thousands of people on the internet each day. With a law degree, I'm probably way overqualified for this position. And I'm definitely still paying back those school loans.

But I'm also a stay-at-home mom who wants to feed my family healthy and nutritious meals. Who wants my girls to grow up knowing that vegetables don't really come from cans and healthy snacks don't come in hundred-calorie packs. Who wants to gather my brood around the dinner table each night and serve them up a nourishing meal that isn't that much different from the comforting home-cooked meals that my mom made for me when I was growing up. Only she didn't care about the lighting. And she didn't rush through the dishes because *The Bachelor* was about to start.

Another obvious difference—my girls, Gigi and Lulu, would rather munch on tofu than chicken nuggets. What can I say? I make some killer tofu. But they fight over Barbies, they plead with me to wear tutus to soccer practice and they never met a Disney princess–emblazoned item of clothing, school supply or beach towel they didn't like.

Sure my husband, Pea Daddy, doesn't eat brats and throw back brewskis during the big game.

But he likes a "manly" meal as much as the next guy, and he'll take down doughnuts with his coffee and sports page on a Sunday morning like it's nobody's business.

Through our blog, for the past three years I've made my family everybody's business. And really, that's the point. Because I see the value in showing the world what a "normal" family we are, tearing down that mind-set that health nuts are just plain nuts.

But what does this mean for you? I don't want you to make drastic overnight changes to fit a label. Nor do I want you necessarily to swear

xi

off meat. But even if you try one or two of these plant-based recipes in this book each week, you can raise the standard by which you feed your family and yourself.

Throughout this book, you'll find these icons at the end of each recipe to help you decipher how best to use these recipes in your everyday cooking.

Freezable
These recipes can be prepared ahead of time and frozen for quick and easy meals.

Veg Value
Based on a series on the blog, these recipes have a low cost per serving and can be made with readily available ingredients that won't break the bank.

Packable
Don't get stuck in the PB and J rut. These recipes are perfect for both kids' and grown-ups' lunch boxes!

Pealightful
Though each recipe includes a detailed nutritional analysis, I've taken the guesswork out by highlighting those recipes that are lower in calories, fat and sugar. They're pealightful!

Wannabe Recipea
From another popular blog series, these recipes are molded after your very favorites. Say hello to your new, healthier recipeas!

My goal with this book was to put together recipes for delicious, comforting, "just so happens to be meat-free" dishes that help us savor every day. It's my absolute joy to share them with you.

meet the peas

Mama Pea
Recipe inventor, storyteller, hair updoer, laundry folder and never-put-awayer. She has retired her flatiron (gasp!), has cut back on the coffee and, just when you didn't think it possible, has dedicated even more of her life to watching young singles find love on prime-time television. Eternal, lasts-forever love.

Pea Daddy
Patient, tolerant and loving husband to Mama Pea and father to Gigi and Lulu. A snob about his root beer, he smuggles his own into the movies rather than drinking what's on tap. But he's always willing to share his drink with an excited little girl, no matter how much kettle corn is stuffed in her mouth. Oh, and he's an ace at laundry putting awaying. Total keeper.

Gigi
Seven-year-old jump-roping, spinach-scarfing, highly dramatic monologue–giving second grader. She is the happiest kid you'll ever meet and has the participation awards to prove it. You'll never find her without a book or without a smile. A very toothless smile.

Lulu

Blond-haired, blue-eyed five-year-old who has a nose for mischief. She's obsessed with puppies, hijacking her mommy's blog, pickles and the naughtiest boy in her Sunday school class. But if you ask her to sum it all up, she'll look you straight in the eye and say, "Cheese is my life." Of course it is.

Pea Kitty

Proof positive that just because you don't eat animals doesn't mean you have to love them. The fuel for the anti–Pea Kitty sentiment is less about the constant hair balls and shredded couch corners and more about the inexplicable lunging attacks at a passerby's ankles. A passerby named Mama Pea. Those knee-high boots aren't just for fashion, kids.

in the peas' pantry

HERE'S A PEEK INTO THE PEA FAMILY CUPBOARDS AND FRIDGE. These are the basic ingredients that I reach for on an (almost) daily basis and that are used throughout the book.

Pantry Basics

AGAVE

ALMOND BUTTER

BAKING STAPLES: Keep on hand essentials like whole wheat pastry flour (see page xix), unbleached organic flour, gluten-free all-purpose flour and xanthan gum (if gluten is an issue), organic sugar, stevia, brown sugar, vanilla and other extracts, instant yeast, baking powder and baking soda.

CANNED BEANS: Garbanzo beans, pinto beans, black beans and black-eyed peas are must-haves. Sure, you can cook dried beans to save money, but it's nice to have your favorites on hand for quick meals.

CANNED PUMPKIN

CANNED TOMATOES: Muir Glen Fire Roasted Diced Tomatoes are my absolute favorite and add a depth of flavor to so many soups and casseroles.

CHIA SEEDS: These tiny dark seeds are rich in omega-3 fatty acids. Chia seeds are a great addition to baked goods, smoothies or puddings. You can find them in your local or chain natural foods stores or online.

CHOCOLATE CHIPS: If you're dairy free, be sure to check the label, but you'll find that many brands, especially the good ones, are dairy free.

COCONUT OIL: Coconut oil is a fine alternative to margarine or butter in baked goods. It has a very faint coconut flavor that goes virtually unnoticed, and it is rich in fatty acids.

COCONUT MILK: Look for unsweetened varieties at your health food store or in the ethnic food aisle of your grocery store. We enjoy the richness of full-fat brands, like Thai Kitchen, but Trader Joe's also sells a very reasonably priced reduced-fat version.

GRAINS: Whole grains, such as brown rice, quinoa, millet and oats, are must-haves.

LENTILS: The brown and red varieties are both nice to have on hand for soups and casseroles.

MAPLE SYRUP

NATURAL PEANUT BUTTER: Skip the big-name brands, which can be full of hydrogenated oils and sugar. Grind your own at the health food store or simply buy ready-made natural brands.

NUTRITIONAL YEAST: A nutritional supplement/condiment made from a deactivated yeast, "nooch" has a nutty, salty, cheesy flavor. It is high in vitamin B12 and protein and is most definitely an acquired taste. You can find it in the spice section of your natural foods store, or look for it in the bulk section and buy it for less and in a smaller quantity.

more peas, thank you

OAT FLOUR: Just like it sounds, this is a flour made from ground oats. You can easily make your own by grinding old-fashioned oats in your blender or food processor.

SPICES: If nothing else, always have a supply of freshly ground cinnamon, chili powder, curry powder, cumin, garlic powder, ginger, nutmeg, onion powder, salt and pepper.

TAHINI

UNSWEETENED APPLESAUCE

VEGETABLE STOCK

WHOLE WHEAT PASTRY FLOUR: This flour has a lower gluten content and the light consistency of traditional all-purpose flour but still has the bran and germ of whole wheat flour, and thus all the nutritional benefits, as well. Cooking with this flour results in lighter and fluffier pancakes, muffins and cookies than those made with regular whole wheat flour.

XANTHAN GUM: A food thickening agent and stabilizer, xanthan gum is great in smoothies and provides structure to gluten-free baked goods. Look for it at natural foods stores.

In the Fridge and Freezer

CONDIMENTS: Line your refrigerator door with all-fruit preserves, organic ketchup (conventionally grown tomatoes are heavily sprayed with pesticides, and many brands contain high-fructose corn syrup), natural barbecue sauce, mustard, reduced sodium soy sauce or tamari (which is gluten free) and vegan mayonnaise (see page xxii).

FLAXSEEDS: Flaxseeds must be ground before consuming, and so you may prefer to buy flax meal or ground flaxseeds. To save money and to keep the flaxseeds fresh longer, you can easily grind your own. Store flaxseeds in the refrigerator to prevent rancidity. For egg-free baking, substitute one tablespoon of ground flaxseeds dissolved in three table-spoons of water for one egg.

LIQUID SMOKE: Look for this in the condiment aisle at your supermarket. It imparts a smoky, almost "bacony" flavor, but without the bacon.

NONDAIRY CHEESES: The cream of the crop in terms of flavor and texture is Daiya, a brand made without soy or casein (milk protein). Daiya can be found at most Whole Foods Markets and some major supermarkets and is available in cheddar, mozzarella and pepper jack varieties.

NONDAIRY MILK: Among the many varieties of nondairy milk available are soy, almond, coconut, rice, oat and hemp. When selecting nondairy milk, pay attention to both the flavor (vanilla doesn't work well in savory recipes) and whether or not the milk is sweetened or unsweetened (some sweetened brands are packed with sugar).

ORGANIC DAIRY PRODUCTS: Organic dairy products are made from milk produced by cows that are 1) fed organic grain; 2) raised in low stress, healthier environments; and 3) not routinely given growth hormones and antibiotics. By choosing organic dairy, you will not just be giving your family a higher quality product, you will be supporting an industry dedicated to preserving the environment and improving the quality of life for farm animals. Organic dairy is becoming cheaper and more commonplace every day, and greater consumer demand for organic dairy products will drive prices down even further. Many supermarkets carry their own lines of organic dairy products, and of course, you can find these products at natural foods stores, as well.

PRODUCE: Always keep on hand organic apples, broccoli, organic celery, carrots, cilantro, frozen bananas, frozen organic blueberries, frozen corn, frozen peas, frozen organic strawberries, garlic, lemons, limes and leafy greens, including organic romaine and organic spinach.

THE DIRTY DOZEN

The Environmental Working Group has named these fruits and vegetables as most likely to have high pesticide residue if grown conventionally. Whenever possible, select organic when you purchase the Dirty Dozen.

- Apples
- Celery
- Sweet bell peppers
- Peaches
- Strawberries
- Nectarines
- Grapes
- Spinach
- Lettuce
- Cucumbers
- Blueberries
- Potatoes

Fruits and vegetables that are peeled before eating, such as bananas and oranges, are perfectly safe even if they are sprayed with pesticides.

TEMPEH

TOFU:

○ FIRM AND EXTRA-FIRM TOFU: These varieties come packaged in water and are found in the refrigerated section of your grocery store. When you order tofu at a restaurant, this is most likely the kind of tofu you'll get. If you drain and press this tofu to remove as much moisture as possible and then marinate it, you can grill it,

HOW TO PRESS TOFU

To press firm or extra-firm tofu, you can buy a tofu press or you can use items found in your kitchen. Open the package, drain the tofu and then slice it into cubes or slabs. If you do not have a tofu press, line a breadboard with a clean tea towel or dishrag. Place the tofu on top of the towel or rag, and then place another clean towel or dishrag on top of the tofu, followed by another bread-board. Stack numerous heavy objects (pans, books, children…) on top of the breadboard, and let the tofu sit for anywhere from twenty minutes to two hours (the longer you press it, the firmer it will become). Prepare the pressed tofu as desired.

bake it and sauté it, just like meat. It has a dense, chewy texture, and personally, we love it.

○ **SILKEN AND SOFT TOFU:** This tofu has the moisture left in the soybean curd and isn't pressed at all. It has a silky texture and can be used in smoothies, puddings and other desserts. It can also be used as a binding agent in cooking or baking. Some brands are shelf stable and don't have to be refrigerated so check the label.

VEGAN CREAM CHEESE: This nondairy spread works well on bagels and toast, and in frostings, baked goods and savory recipes. Tofutti Better Than Cream Cheese is readily available in most natural foods stores.

VEGAN MARGARINE: This nondairy margarine is used as a spread and in cooking. The most popular and readily available brand is Earth Balance.

VEGAN MAYONNAISE: This egg-free, dairy-free spread is used on sandwiches and in dips and salad dressings. The most popular and readily available brand is Vegenaise.

VEGAN WORCESTERSHIRE SAUCE: While traditional Worcestershire sauce contains anchovies, vegan varieties are fish free. Annie's Naturals Organic Worcestershire Sauce is a popular brand.

Substitutions

I SEE FOOD CHOICES AS BEING INTENSELY PERSONAL. The motivation behind what we eat or don't eat can be based on a myriad of health issues or personal ethics. We should respect each individual's right to make those choices for him- or herself.

That having been said, I wanted to provide some across-the-board substitutions for ingredients that are commonly avoided for those readers who wish to use these recipes and modify them so that they are in line with their own choices. No judgment—just options.

SUGAR: For those individuals watching their sugar intake, you may substitute stevia for at least a portion of the sugar used in the desserts and sweets recipes. You can also purchase stevia baking blends, such as those made by NuNaturals, which make a pretty seamless substitution across the board. If you would prefer to use agave or maple syrup instead of sugar, for each cup of white or brown sugar called for in the recipe, use $\frac{2}{3}$ cup of agave or maple syrup and reduce the other liquids in the recipe by $\frac{1}{4}$ to $\frac{1}{3}$ cup.

DAIRY PRODUCTS: For those individuals who consume dairy products, you can use those products in place of the nondairy products mentioned in the recipes. I encourage you to find organic and local dairy sources, for the reasons discussed previously. Please note that with some recipes, you will get a slightly different texture if you use butter in place of vegan margarine or coconut oil. This is especially true with cookies made with butter, which will spread more easily upon baking, as well as with other baked goods.

GLUTEN: For gluten-free readers, you can successfully substitute all-purpose gluten-free flour in most of the recipes. I recommend adding $\frac{1}{4}$ to $\frac{1}{2}$ teaspoon xanthan gum to help with leavening. Some gluten-free flours to consider using as well are brown rice flour and oat flour made from gluten-free oats.

Breakfasts

Sunrise Smoothies 2

Strawberry Multigrain
Cereal Bars 5

Oatmeal Cookie Granola 8

PB and J Smoothies 11

Tempeh Bacon 14

Time-Saving Tofu
Scramble Spice Blend 16

Pumpkin
Cheesecake Muffins 18

Cherry Oat Scones 21

Lemon Chia Pancakes 24

Home Fries 26

Peach Cornmeal Muffins ... 29

Cheddar "Bacon"
Scones 32

Creamy Power Porridge 35

Easy Apple Oat Cakes 38

Pineapple
Upside-Down Muffins 40

Maple Apple Spice
Coffee Cake 43

Pumpkin Cinnamon
Rolls 45

Sunrise Smoothies

Makes 4 smoothies

HAVE YOU HEARD OF THAT CHILDREN'S BOOK (THAT ISN'T FOR CHILDREN) CALLED *GO THE F**K TO SLEEP?*

The book is so very, very wrong. And so very, very funny. I've already got the follow-up book concept sketched out in my head. It's called *Why the H**l Are You Up?*

This morning I treasured the thought of "sleeping in" after a long, tiring week. I put "sleeping in" in quotes because if you are childless that could mean sleeping until ten or eleven in the morning, but once your womb has been compromised, so has that term.

"Sleeping in."

I'd just like to sleep until it's no longer dark outside. Is that too much to ask?

Sometime around dawn, a little head peeked into my bedroom, the door squeaking ever so slightly. Then a big mass of curls attached to a little body burst in the room violently. I'm pretty sure her hair opened the door by itself.

I escorted The Hair back to her room, asking as nicely as I could muster, "Why are you up?"

She looked at me thoughtfully and asked, "Are there owls in Oregon?"

"Yes. Why?"

"I think an owl woke me up," she answered.

"No, Geeg, the owls are asleep," I said jealously, hoping Mrs. Williams hadn't been so ambitious as to teach her about nocturnal animals in kindergarten.

"Well, then it was the washing machine," she replied, trying again.

I scowled and said, "Nice try, kid, but you know I haven't done laundry in at least two weeks, and there's no way I'm doing it at five forty-five."

She sized up my pajamas/workout clothes outfit, which I'd been wearing for the past twenty-four hours. Don't judge.

A lightbulb went off. "I know! It was the treadmill!"

"Nope, kid. I was asleep."

"Well, maybe I was just excited to go to the beach with Mimi and Poppy tomorrow."

Bingo.

I gave up any hope of either one of us going back to bed, so we got up, went downstairs, colored in *My Little Pony* coloring books with scratchy, worn-out markers and tried to giggle quietly so as not to wake the rest of the house. As I passed her a marker, I said, "I understand, Geeg. You just really like spending time with Mimi and Poppy. I'd get up early for that too."

And then she twisted a curl around her green marker–stained finger and looked up at me and said, "Actually, Mom, I like spending time with you."

All I could say to that was, "Cheers."

INGREDIENTS

1½ cups frozen strawberries

1½ cups apple juice

stevia, honey or agave to taste (optional)

1 cup frozen mango

½ cup frozen pineapple

1½ cups orange juice

4 strawberries, to garnish (optional)

DIRECTIONS

1   In a blender, combine strawberries, apple juice and sweetener, if using.

2   Pour strawberry smoothie carefully into 4 glasses, and transfer glasses to freezer for 10 to 15 minutes to allow strawberry layer to set.

3   Rinse out blender and put in mango, pineapple, orange juice and sweetener, if using. Blend until smooth. Remove glasses from freezer and carefully pour mango smoothie into each one to achieve a layered effect.

4   Garnish with a fresh strawberry and serve.

NUTRITION INFORMATION PER SERVING: 150 calories, 0 g total fat, 0 g saturated fat, 0 g trans fat, 0 mg cholesterol, 5 mg sodium, 39 g carbohydrate, 4 g fiber, 30 g sugar, 1 g protein, vitamin A 8%, vitamin C 130%, calcium 4%, iron 6%

Optional ingredients and toppings not included in analysis.

pea points

The longer you let the strawberry layer set, the more distinct the divide will be between the layers. You can also make these in Popsicle molds for a two-tone frozen summer treat.

more peas, thank you

Strawberry Multigrain Cereal Bars

Makes 8 bars

These bars were inspired by those prepackaged, "nutritious" cereal bars that we all grew up on. Only these have eight ingredients instead of forty-eight.

I GAVE UP MY GYM MEMBERSHIP SEVEN YEARS AGO.

I think pretty much every day of those seven years has been filled with regret.

It's not because I've packed on the pounds. I actually wouldn't know—the only scale I ever used was at the gym. That scale evidently was owned by an elderly woman in a blue Speedo, though, because every time I felt the old jeans getting a little tight and wanted to hop on, she'd already set up camp there. Sans the Speedo. And suddenly I felt just fine about my jeans and pretty much became a fan of all clothing in general.

It's not because I miss my personal trainer, Dave, and how he told me every week that I was his favorite client. I have no delusions. He was just using me for my cookies, which I'm perfectly okay with since I could talk him out of sprints with gingersnaps. Snickerdoodles saved me from lunges. Cookie dough balls got me out of some squats. You get the picture. I was just throwing my money away and making the best personal trainer in town chubby. But I never had to do pull-ups, either.

I don't have an excuse to buy cute gym clothes anymore, since the only people who see them care only if my sports bra is pink. Thank goodness I bought that fuchsia number on clearance seven years ago, and thank goodness Gigi and Lulu are oblivious to holes and frayed elastic. At least it's *pink* frayed elastic. And just last week I worked out in a dirty old baseball cap, a bikini top, flannel boxers and Pea Daddy's tube socks. I need to do laundry.

My regret in quitting the gym has more to do with the built-in audience in the living room. My little cheering squad is right there to root me on every morning, when I pop in my workout DVDs, whether I want them to be or not.

One of my favorite DVD workouts is led by a Norwegian fitness model. She has the face of a supermodel on the body of a professional wrestler. A *male* professional wrestler. As a result, the girls are terrified of her, and frankly, so am I. She's degrading and insulting, spewing insults in broken English. "Don't quit now. You like a cottage cheese merin-gay!" I don't even know what a "cottage cheese merin-gay" is, but I'm pretty sure I don't want to be one.

More than the personal attacks, though, I'm bothered by her obsession with the word *butt,* a word I've worked very hard to eliminate from my children's vocabulary, especially when one of my angels used it to get her sister to stop poking her in the middle of church on Sunday.

But even after we get over the initial fear and potty talk, I still can't do my DVD workout without a whole lot of cracks coming from the kitchen table.

"Mom! Why are you using those little weights when she's using the big ones?"

"Mom! Why is she doing push-ups on her toes and you're doing them on your knees?"

"Mom! Why are you lying on the floor, panting, you cottage cheese merin-gay?"

I've got a new strategy these days, though, and it involves distraction. Before I push Play, I hand out some cereal bars. And just like my trainer, no one can complain with their mouth full.

INGREDIENTS

1½ cups whole wheat pastry flour

2½ cups old-fashioned oats

2 teaspoons baking powder

½ teaspoon salt

¼ cup vegan margarine (i.e., Earth Balance) or organic butter, melted

¼ cup organic sugar

½ cup unsweetened applesauce

cooking spray, to grease baking pan

1⅓ cups 100 percent fruit strawberry preserves

DIRECTIONS

1   Preheat oven to 375 degrees F.

2   In a large bowl, combine flour, oats, baking powder and salt. In a smaller bowl, combine melted margarine or butter, sugar and applesauce.

3   Add the applesauce mixture to the dry ingredients, and stir until fully moistened. Press half of the mixture into the bottom of an 8 x 8-inch baking pan that has been sprayed with cooking spray.

4   Spread preserves over the bottom crust. Place the remaining mixture on top of the preserves and press down to form the top crust. Bake for 20 to 25 minutes, until the top is golden brown.

5   Cool completely before cutting into bars.

NUTRITION INFORMATION PER SERVING: 320 calories, 8 g total fat, 2 g saturated fat, 0 g trans fat, 0 mg cholesterol, 290 mg sodium, 59 g carbohydrate, 5 g fiber, 25 g sugar, 5 g protein, vitamin A 0%, vitamin C 2%, calcium 0%, iron 10%

Oatmeal Cookie Granola

Makes approximately 10 servings of ⅔ cup each

IF I HAD TO PICK ONE OF MY FAVORITE PLACES ON EARTH, IT WOULDN'T BE A SUNNY BEACH, MY CHILDHOOD PLAYHOUSE OR EVEN MY GRANDMA'S KITCHEN.

No, my favorite place on Earth has to be the grocery store. I should point out that both my dad and his mom worked at grocery stores, so I associate blue, crisp grocers' aprons with my amah and the smell of her perfume as she gave me a tight hug. Just the beep of the grocery scanner reminds me of my dad's soothing voice saying, "You're here? I'll take a break" as he led us into the back room with sodas and loaded price-marking guns.

Even though I had a front row seat to all the inner workings of the supermarket, that wasn't even my favorite part of growing up in the store.

I loved the aisles.

The perfectly faced, fully stocked aisles with their gleaming floors just waiting for me. And you.

The best aisle of all was the cereal aisle. Never mind that my mom only ever bought Cheerios, Rice Krispies and Kix, because they had three grams of sugar or less. Those and the occasional box of higher in sugar Raisin Bran, but it had both raisins and bran, so there was nothing to actually celebrate. Still, my brother and I loved to scope out the aisle, hoping that if we pestered my mother enough, it would pay off. She wouldn't cave and buy us the sugary cereal, but often she'd be so frazzled, she'd need a weekend away with my father. They'd send us off to Amah, who would take us to "work" and let us pick out whatever glorious, delicious cereal with thirty-two grams of sugar we wanted.

I always chose Franken Berry, and for one reason alone: pink milk. My brother was really the smart one, though (or maybe just the victim of clever marketing), because he always picked Cookie Crisp. Even though I loved my pink milk, I was always jealous of my brother's huge, heaping

bowl of cookies for breakfast. It's a cereal made of cookies! Can you imagine? Tell me that's not a healthy part of a balanced breakfast.

I'm not even sure if they make Cookie Crisp anymore. You'd think some irate, nutrition-crazed mommy blogger would have gotten her drawers in a bunch and called for a nationwide ban on the stuff by now. Or maybe she'd use it as inspiration.

This granola does not resemble Cookie Crisp at all. But it does have a few things going for it: it tastes like a fresh baked oatmeal cookie and it is a cereal with *cookie* in the title. And though you don't get a trip to one of my favorite places in the world to get it, it's almost as easy to go whip up a batch.

INGREDIENTS

5 cups old-fashioned oats

1½ cups roasted or raw almonds, chopped

2 teaspoons cinnamon

½ teaspoon ground ginger

½ teaspoon nutmeg

¼ teaspoon salt

¼ cup honey

¼ cup maple syrup

½ cup organic raisins

pea points

While this cereal is great served with almond milk, we love a handful sprinkled on top of a smoothie or even just straight out of the container while we're on the go.

DIRECTIONS

1 Preheat oven to 350 degrees F.

2 In a large bowl, combine oats, almonds, cinnamon, ginger, nutmeg and salt. In a smaller bowl, mix together honey and maple syrup. Pour syrup mixture over oat mixture and stir until evenly coated.

3 Spread granola on a baking sheet and bake for 25 to 30 minutes, or until cereal is toasted, stirring every 10 minutes during baking.

4 Stir in raisins and allow granola to cool completely before storing in an airtight container in the refrigerator for up to several weeks.

NUTRITION INFORMATION PER SERVING: 310 calories, 10 g total fat, 1 g saturated fat, 0 g trans fat, 0 mg cholesterol, 60 mg sodium, 49 g carbohydrate, 6 g fiber, 19 g sugar, 8 g protein, vitamin A 0%, vitamin C 2%, calcium 6%, iron 15%

more peas, thank you

PB and J Smoothies

Makes 4 smoothies of approximately 1½ cups each

I'M HAUNTED BY PEANUT BUTTER AND JELLY SANDWICHES.

Until the age of thirteen, I loved a good old PB and J as much as the next kid. I wasn't picky—creamy or crunchy, wheat or white, crusted or decrusted—I'd eat it.

But then I became an entrepreneur. The summer between seventh and eighth grade my dad's coworker at the Thriftway asked if I'd want to come babysit his kids every day for three months. I quickly did the math and realized that at five dollars an hour, five days a week, every day for three months, I'd be rich. Or at least able to afford the tickets to the New Kids on the Block concert I'd been coveting. *Hangin' Tough* for life.

I was nervous when I arrived at the family's house that first day, and rightfully so. As soon as I turned the handle on that very normal-looking front door, I opened a portal to a dark, dark place. A portal so evil that once opened, it could never be closed. And I have never been the same.

The house was cluttered, with clothes lying on the floor, next to empty dresser drawers, toys missing batteries, battery packages missing batteries, crayons escaped from their boxes, loose change, beach towels and newspapers. And mysteriously, there amid the clutter was the slightly petrified crust from a peanut butter and jelly sandwich.

The only thing the mom in this household was more challenged at than cleaning was cooking. So I wasn't terribly surprised when she directed me to the kitchen, showed me a loaf of Wonder Bread, a jar of Skippy and one of grape Smucker's and told me this was lunch. And it was. Every day for three months.

Now, if I were smart, I would have started packing a lunch for myself come July. But I wasn't smart. I was thirteen and was too busy believing that somehow if Jordan Knight saw me in the front row at his concert, he would cut off that awful rattail and ask me to leave the eighth grade and come on tour with him and the New Kids. It could have happened.

The poor kids seemed oblivious to the fact that there was anything else they possibly could have eaten for lunch. They also seemed oblivious to the fact that there were things like toy boxes, laundry hampers and, astonishingly enough, garbage cans in their very own home.

The summer came and went. The New Kids came and went. And by the time school started and my job ended, seventy-eight peanut butter and jelly sandwiches later, I never wanted to eat another PB and J again.

But a PB and J Smoothie? That's an entirely different creature. And there's no pesky crust to throw away, either.

INGREDIENTS

2⅔ cups nondairy milk or organic milk

2⅔ cups frozen organic strawberries

⅓ cup unsalted natural peanut butter

1 cup old-fashioned oats

½ teaspoon salt

agave nectar or stevia to taste

chopped peanuts, to garnish (optional)

pea points

For an extra protein boost, add in some vanilla protein powder. This protein-enhanced smoothie is an amazing post-workout treat.

DIRECTIONS

Combine milk, strawberries, peanut butter, oats, salt and sweetener in a high-speed blender. Blend until smooth and thick. Adjust sweetener to taste, pour in glasses and serve, garnishing with chopped peanuts, if desired.

NUTRITION INFORMATION PER SERVING: 310 calories, 14 g total fat, 3 g saturated fat, 0 g trans fat, 5 mg cholesterol, 380 mg sodium, 34 g carbohydrate, 6 g fiber, 6 g sugar, 14 g protein, vitamin A 6%, vitamin C 110%, calcium 25%, iron 10%

Optional ingredients and toppings not included in analysis.

Tempeh Bacon

Makes 8 slices
This tempeh bacon is similar in flavor and texture to the store brands but is
easier on your wallet and has fewer ingredients.

IT SEEMS AS THOUGH BACON IS A BIG OBSTACLE IN GETTING MEAT
EATERS TO DEVOTE THEMSELVES TO A PLANT-BASED DIET.

"I could be a vegetarian if it weren't for bacon," people explain. Chef
Tal Ronnen has famously said, "Then be a vegetarian that eats bacon!"
arguing that any reduction in meat consumption is a step toward saving
the lives of animals.

No matter where you fall on the meat-eating spectrum, here's a tasty
alternative to regular bacon that we just can't get enough of.

INGREDIENTS

1 8-ounce package tempeh

2 tablespoons maple syrup

1½ tablespoons olive oil

1½ teaspoons liquid smoke

1 teaspoon vegan Worcestershire
sauce

2 tablespoons reduced sodium
soy sauce

1 teaspoon onion powder

1 teaspoon garlic powder

cooking spray or oil,
to grease skillet

DIRECTIONS

1   Set tempeh on a cutting board, and grab a sharp knife. Slice
    tempeh lengthwise as thinly as possible, but not so thin that
    your strips break. You should be able to get 8 strips out of one
    block of tempeh.

2   In a large shallow baking dish or pie plate, combine maple syrup,
    oil, liquid smoke, Worcestershire sauce, soy sauce, onion powder
    and garlic powder, and whisk together well.

3   Place tempeh strips in marinade, cover and refrigerate for anywhere
    from an hour to overnight.

more peas, thank you

4 Place a skillet that has been coated with cooking spray or oil over medium-high heat. Lay strips of tempeh in the skillet, cooking in batches of 4 slices. Cook for 2 to 3 minutes on each side, or until tempeh is crisp and browned.

NUTRITION INFORMATION PER SERVING: 90 calories, 3.5 g total fat, 0.5 g saturated fat, 0 g trans fat, 0 mg cholesterol, 160 mg sodium, 9 g carbohydrate, <1 g fiber, 4 g sugar, 4 g protein, vitamin A 0%, vitamin C 0%, calcium 4%, iron 4 %

Time-Saving Tofu Scramble Spice Blend

Makes 2 cups of mix

I LOVE BREAKFAST FOR DINNER.

It's the ultimate shortcut on those nights when I don't have the energy or time to mix up something elaborate and we're plumb out of leftovers. It happens.

But I don't always want a tummy full of syrupy pancakes or frosted doughnuts before bed. Okay, I do, but I have to set a good example. The perfect solution? A nice tofu scramble. It's flavorful, filling, full of protein and makes scrambled eggs quiver with fear that they've been replaced for good.

I love the basic tofu scramble recipe that is featured in *Peas and Thank You.* But I'm always looking for a shortcut. And a jar of this spice blend is just that.

There are a few staples that are always in my fridge: almond milk, carrots, broccoli, tofu, Gigi's spinach, Pea Daddy's root beer and Lulu's pickles, naturally.

Add a jar of this seasoning to the list. It keeps forever, and it makes preparing a tofu scramble for breakfast a cinch. Or dinner, depending on the day of the week. Or *days* of the week. It happens.

INGREDIENTS

Tofu Seasoning Spice Blend:
1½ tablespoons turmeric

¼ cup cumin

¼ cup curry powder

2 tablespoons garlic powder

2 tablespoons onion powder

⅔ cup nutritional yeast

¼ cup dried parsley

1½ tablespoons salt

Tofu Scramble:
1 16-ounce block organic firm or extra firm tofu

3 tablespoons Tofu Seasoning Spice Blend

cooking spray or oil, to grease skillet

DIRECTIONS

1   To make the spice blend, I combine all ingredients in a jar or a resealable container.

2   Drain the tofu, crumble it, gently squeeze out the excess liquid and pat dry. In a medium bowl, add the crumbled tofu, 3 tablespoons of the spice blend and toss tofu until evenly coated.

3   To make the tofu scramble, heat a skillet that has been coated with cooking spray or oil over medium-high heat.

4   Sauté tofu in the hot skillet for about 10 to 12 minutes. I like to leave it alone for several minutes at a time, letting it get a bit brown and crispy, before stirring it again and then letting it get firmer and browner.

5   Serve hot. Store remaining spice blend covered in the fridge for as long as several weeks.

NUTRITION INFORMATION PER SERVING: 5 calories, 0 g total fat, 0 g saturated fat, 0 g trans fat, 0 mg cholesterol, 110 mg sodium, <1 g carbohydrate, 0 g fiber, 0 g sugar, <1 g protein, vitamin A 0%, vitamin C 0%, calcium 0%, iron 0%

Based on 96 servings of 1 teaspoon each.

Pumpkin Cheesecake Muffins

Makes 12 muffins

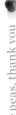

NECESSITY IS THE MOTHER OF INVENTION, AND THERE ARE TRULY TIMES IN MY LIFE WHEN I NEED CHEESECAKE FOR BREAKFAST.

And then there are other times, like those two short hours per week when both girls are at school, Pea Daddy is at work and Pea Kitty is upstairs, hawking up a hair ball on our duvet cover, when I *really* need cheesecake for breakfast.

But it's not something I *should* do.

My friend Deb has been talking to me a lot lately about the word *should*. Since she's smarter than I am, I listen when she gives advice, even if I have to fight with every fiber of my being not to let certain things about her affect our friendship.

And by that I mean, if I didn't love her so much, I would hate her.

Because she has glossy, silky hair without the aid of flatirons and hair spray. (Guilty as charged, ozone layer.) Because she bakes every slice of bread that ever crosses her children's lips. (And my kids would rather eat her bread than just about anything. Except dough balls.) Because she runs farther in her weekly three-hour Saturday run than I do in a month. (Even if a hungry tiger was chasing me, I'd last only twenty minutes. But I'd still need a strategically planned playlist.)

Because in our Bible study, which *I* started months ago, she's on week twelve in our workbook and I'm still on day two. (Sorry, God. Love you. Don't ever change.)

I said to Deb, "I'll catch up. I know I *should*."

And she turns to me with that sweet face of hers and says, "Sarah, don't do things just because you *should*. The word *should* is loaded with judgment. The things that really are important to you feel so good when you do them that you *want* to do them. Get rid of *should*."

Do you see why I'm willing to overlook the fact that she reads history books for fun and has never watched an episode of *The Bachelorette* in her life?

So I don't say that I made these muffins even though I should come up with a better alternative to breakfast than cheesecake. I say that I made them because pumpkin cheesecake muffins are important to me and I feel so good when I eat them that I want to make them.

I hope you will, too. (Because you really *should*.)

INGREDIENTS

12 paper muffin baking cups or cooking spray to grease muffin tin

1 cup whole wheat pastry flour

½ cup unbleached all-purpose flour

½ teaspoon baking soda

1½ teaspoons nutmeg

2 teaspoons cinnamon

½ teaspoon salt

1 cup canned pumpkin

⅓ cup organic milk or nondairy milk

½ cup organic sugar

1 teaspoon vanilla extract

½ cup nondairy cream cheese (i.e., Tofutti) or organic cream cheese

½ cup powdered sugar

DIRECTIONS

1 Preheat oven to 350 degrees F. Line a 12-cup muffin tin with paper baking cups or spray with cooking spray and set aside.

2 In a large bowl, combine flours, baking soda, nutmeg, cinnamon and salt.

3 In a medium bowl or a large liquid measuring cup, combine pumpkin, milk, sugar and ½ teaspoon of the vanilla extract.

4 Add pumpkin mixture to dry ingredients and stir until just combined.

5 Using an electric mixer, beat together cream cheese, powdered sugar and the remaining ½ teaspoon of vanilla. Do not overbeat.

6 Fill each muffin cup ⅓ of the way full with pumpkin batter. Top the batter in each cup with a spoonful of cheesecake filling and then top the filling with an additional scoop of pumpkin batter. Each cup should be three-quarters full.

7 Spread the batter out with a small spoon or your finger so that the cheesecake filling is completely covered.

8 Bake muffins for 23 to 25 minutes, or until they are golden and have set.

NUTRITION INFORMATION PER SERVING: 130 calories, 3 g total fat, 0.5 g saturated fat, 0 g trans fat, 0 mg cholesterol, 230 mg sodium, 25 g carbohydrate, 2 g fiber, 12 g sugar, 2 g protein, vitamin A 60%, vitamin C 2%, calcium 2%, iron 4%

more peas, thank you

Cherry Oat Scones

Makes 8 scones

IF YOU'VE NEVER MADE HOMEMADE SCONES, YOU REALLY MUST. DON'T BE INTIMIDATED—IT IS EVER SO EASY.

I'm not just going to tell you how easy it is, though. I'm going to prove it to you.

The evidence: I created these scones on a recent Sunday morning, while doing some serious multitasking. Gigi was acting out the first Christmas. In her groundbreaking show, she was Gabriel, Mary, Joseph and a donkey, and in a Christmas miracle, she also played a shrieking Baby Jesus. Although, according to "Away in a Manger," the little Lord Jesus "no crying he makes." She needs to work on her historical accuracy.

Amid the Nativity scene, Lulu was sitting in the middle of our very small kitchen floor, between my feet. Inexplicably, every thirty seconds or so, she'd let out an eardrum-shattering, "Quack!"

"And unto you…quack…a child shall be born, and he shall be Lord… quack…of all."

Amid the coming of our Lord and the coming of our duck, Pea Daddy was sitting at the kitchen counter, in my "office," the three-by-three-foot space that houses my laptop and a bar stool. He was telling me some tale of fantasy football woe, something to do with some other team's quarterback mistakenly not starting this week. I really couldn't tell you what he was saying, because I really wasn't listening. I pretty much tune out after the word *fantasy*.

"And so Mary and Joseph traveled by donkey…quack…. They sat out Carson Palmer, and I have no idea why…. And all of the inns were full, so they settled into a warm stable…quack…which is fine by me, since because of their flub, my team moved up to first place…quack!"

See my point? If I can make these scones amid the coming of our Lord, the coming of our duck and the coming of a mind-numbing fake sports scenario, you can handle making these for breakfast.

I just hope you have better luck than I do when you try to eat them in peace.

Heavenly, heavenly peace. Quack!

INGREDIENTS

Cooking spray, to grease baking sheet

⅓ cup nondairy milk or organic milk

1 teaspoon lemon juice

1 cup whole wheat pastry flour

½ cup unbleached all-purpose flour

½ teaspoon baking soda

1 teaspoon baking powder

½ teaspoon salt

1 teaspoon nutmeg

¼ cup vegan margarine (i.e., Earth Balance), coconut oil or organic butter

1 cup old-fashioned oats

½ cup unsweetened dried cherries, chopped

¼ cup unsweetened applesauce

⅓ cup light brown sugar

2 teaspoons vanilla extract

1 tablespoon organic sugar for sprinkling (optional)

DIRECTIONS

1 Preheat oven to 350 degrees F. Lightly grease or spray a baking sheet with cooking spray.

2 In a small bowl or a large liquid measuring cup, combine milk and lemon juice and set aside. This effectively curdles your milk.

3 In a large bowl, combine flours, baking soda, baking powder, salt and nutmeg. Cut in margarine, coconut oil or butter until the flour mixture has the texture of wet sand. Fold in oats and cherries.

4 To the milk mixture, add applesauce, brown sugar and vanilla. Add milk mixture to flour mixture and fold until just combined.

5 Turn dough out onto a lightly floured surface, and knead briefly. Roll or pat dough into a 1-inch thick round. Cut into 8 wedges, and place them 2 inches apart on a baking sheet. Sprinkle wedges with the tablespoon of sugar, if desired.

6 Bake 20 to 23 minutes, or until golden brown on the bottom.

NUTRITION INFORMATION PER SERVING: 240 calories, 7 g total fat, 2 g saturated fat, 0 g trans fat, 0 mg cholesterol, 290 mg sodium, 40 g carbohydrate, 3 g fiber, 14 g sugar, 4 g protein, vitamin A 0%, vitamin C 2%, calcium 2%, iron 6%

Optional ingredients and toppings not included in analysis.

Lemon Chia Pancakes

Makes 12 6-inch pancakes

I'M NOT ONE TO BRAG, BUT THESE MIGHT VERY WELL BE THE BEST PANCAKES I'VE EVER HAD.

If that doesn't encourage you to zest a lemon, whip up these pancakes and make snow slopes of powdered sugar on top, I don't know what will.

But I'll give you a few more reasons, anyway:

1 You like your family. You may even love them. But you want them to stop jump roping in the hallway, finger painting with applesauce on the coffee table and telling you once again about who they hope to select in their fantasy basketball/baseball/football draft that is going to occur later today. (Hint: people can't jump rope, finger paint or talk about their fantasies when their mouths are full of pancakes.)

2 You really want to eat a lemon bar for breakfast but realize that shortbread and lemon curd generally shouldn't be eaten before noon.

3 You appreciate that poppy seeds are a gateway drug. Just say no. (This advice also applies to any form of jumping in the house, using food for art and playing "pretend" with professional athletes.)

4 You have a big bag of chia seeds that you bought and have no clue what to do with. Making a paste and spreading it over a ceramic cat is actually starting to sound appealing. (Ch-ch-ch-chia!)

5 You have a griddle and thus the luxury of making eight pancakes at a time. I'd like to borrow that. I haven't had a hot pancake since 2004.

6 You are out of chocolate chips, rendering it impossible to make chocolate chip pancakes. If you are out of chocolate chips, you have bigger issues than what you should eat for breakfast. Get yourself to the store immediately.

But first make these pancakes.

INGREDIENTS

1 cup whole wheat pastry flour

1 cup unbleached all-purpose flour

2 teaspoons baking powder

½ teaspoon baking soda

½ teaspoon salt

1 tablespoon organic sugar

½ cup unsweetened applesauce

1½ cups nondairy milk or organic milk

2 tablespoons fresh lemon juice

2 teaspoons lemon zest

1½ tablespoons chia seeds

cooking spray or oil, to grease skillet

vegan margarine or organic dairy butter and powdered sugar, to garnish

DIRECTIONS

1   In a large bowl, combine flours, baking powder, baking soda, salt and sugar. In a medium-size bowl, combine applesauce, milk and lemon juice.

2   Add milk mixture to dry ingredients and lightly stir until just combined. Fold in lemon zest and chia seeds.

3   Heat a skillet or griddle that has been greased with cooking spray or oil over medium heat. For each pancake, pour approximately ¼ cup batter into the skillet. Cook for several minutes, until the bottom is golden and bubbles have formed on the surface of each pancake. Flip pancakes and cook for an additional 1 to 2 minutes, or until golden.

4   Serve with vegan margarine or organic dairy butter and a dusting of powdered sugar.

NUTRITION INFORMATION PER SERVING: 110 calories, 1.5 g total fat, 0 g saturated fat, 0 g trans fat, 0 mg cholesterol, 190 mg sodium, 21 g carbohydrate, 3 g fiber, 4 g sugar, 4 g protein, vitamin A 2%, vitamin C 4%, calcium 6%, iron 4%

pea points

I always double my pancake recipe when I'm whipping up a batch on the weekends. Save leftovers in the freezer and pop them in the toaster for a quick breakfast on busy mornings.

Breakfasts

Home Fries

Serves 4
These home fries are just like those you'd find at a diner or campground,
only they are better enjoyed in the comfort of your home.

**I'M SURE THERE WILL PROBABLY COME A DAY, PERHAPS IN ABOUT
TEN YEARS OR SO, WHEN MY GIRLS TURN ON ME.**

I will explain that Gigi and Lulu are far better nicknames than Muff.
Thanks, Mom. I will defend their attacks with convincing evidence of how
I got up for nighttime feedings, kissed boo-boos and wore maternity
clothes well into their toddlerhood so we could pay for diapers. And,
well, because elastic waistbands are comfy. And if they still need proof
that they were loved, I will pull out all the stops and share with them the
ultimate sign of my affection: I have never taken them camping.

Obviously, my parents were punishing me for something by taking
us camping every summer. There's no other explanation for leaving our
warm, dry house with conveniences like mattresses and floors not made
out of dirt. There's no other explanation for abandoning running water,
doors with locks, which keep bears and serial killers away, and even a
room to go to the bathroom in that doesn't have a giant, stinky hole filled
with other people's crap in it. I can still smell that outhouse, the campfire
smoke in my hair and my two brothers after not having bathed for a week.

The only proof my mom wasn't trying to kill me with these great family
"vacations" was the fact that she fed us. And fed us well. What they say is
right—food just always tastes better in the outdoors. That's because you are
so miserable that any hint of warmth, nourishment and pleasure is welcome.

But my mom's fried potatoes were just that—pleasure. Crispy and filling, I can still hear them frying in the skillet while the river rushes behind
our tents, still damp from the morning dew. Also damp were my feet,
purple with cold. That three-mile hike warmed me up in no time. Especially
when our dog got off his leash and ran all the way down the mountain,
my whole family tearing behind him, oblivious to the whir of our fishing
rods caught in trees and the line tearing out behind us.

Sheer panic also kept me warm, like when my older brother hit my younger brother in the head with a rock while my parents were on a firewood run. Nothing an hour's drive to the nearest hospital and five stitches couldn't fix, only so that we could return again for another four days in the wilderness. But those fried potatoes really take the edge off of sheer terror and misery.

This recipe is pretty close to my mom's, but with one big difference. Thankfully, now we can all enjoy them at home.

Mommy loves you, girls.

INGREDIENTS

1¾ pounds Yukon Gold potatoes, cut into 1-inch cubes

cooking spray or oil, to grease skillet

1 medium yellow onion, diced

1 organic red bell pepper, seeded, deveined and diced

1 tablespoon vegan margarine (i.e., Earth Balance), coconut oil or organic butter

salt and pepper to taste

DIRECTIONS

1   Bring a large pot of water to a boil and add potatoes. Boil for 8 to 9 minutes, or until potatoes just begin to soften. Alternatively, place potatoes in a large microwave-safe bowl, add a tablespoon of water and cover bowl tightly with a plate. Microwave for 2 to 3 minutes, shake bowl (without removing cover) to toss potatoes and microwave for an additional 2 to 3 minutes, or until potatoes just begin to soften.

2   Meanwhile, grease a large skillet with cooking spray or oil and place over medium heat. Add onion and red pepper and cook until softened and starting to brown, about 6 minutes. Transfer to a small bowl and set aside.

3   Melt vegan margarine, coconut oil or butter in the skillet and return to medium heat. Add potatoes and pack down with spatula. Cook, without disturbing, until the bottoms of the potatoes are brown, about 5 to 7 minutes. Turn potatoes, pack down again, and continue to cook until undersides are crisp and nicely browned, about 5 to 7 minutes. Reduce heat to medium-low. Stir potatoes every 3 minutes for an additional 9 to 12 minutes, or until evenly browned and crispy on all sides.

4   Return sautéed onions and peppers to the skillet and stir. Season with salt and pepper to taste.

pea points

Switch things up by replacing the Yukon Gold potatoes in this recipe with sweet potatoes or even other root vegetables, like parsnips, carrots or turnips.

NUTRITION INFORMATION PER SERVING: 200 calories, 3 g total fat, 1 g saturated fat, 0 g trans fat, 0 mg cholesterol, 40 mg sodium, 41 g carbohydrate, 6 g fiber, 5 g sugar, 5 g protein, vitamin A 25%, vitamin C 200%, calcium 4%, iron 10%

more peas, thank you

Peach Cornmeal Muffins

Makes 12 muffins

SOMEWHERE ALONG THE WAY, MY WHOLE STRATEGY OF HAVING PEA DADDY FEED THE GIRLS BREAKFAST ON WEEKDAYS WENT AWRY.

Though we are truly equals as parents, I am truly a control freak who likes to tell people what to do. (Keep reading this book. Then go buy a second and third copy for your mom and your best friend.)

Breakfast each morning becomes a test of my willpower to keep my big fat trap shut. As I'm spending those few minutes I call my own each day either grunting with dumbbells or, better yet, making an investment in some personal grooming, I can't help but peek in on the process.

"What do you guys want for breakfast?" Pea Daddy asks eagerly.

"Corn bread," Gigi says.

I expect Pea Daddy to shoot her down with a bagel or oatmeal.

"With lots of honey, right?"

No such luck.

"And what do you want, Lu?" he asks, as she has worked her way onto the kitchen counter, unplugged my phone, beat two levels of Angry Birds and is now watching a puppy popping balloons on YouTube.

"Corn bread," she says without even looking up. But then, as if she's suddenly remembered something important, like breakfast is the most important meal of the day, she looks up and urgently adds, "With a pickle on the side."

"Coming right up!" says my amenable coparent.

You know I'm loosening up in my old age when I don't even say a word. And Pea Daddy proceeds to hand our growing young children corn bread and pickles for breakfast. I may not say anything, but sometimes baked goods speak louder than words.

These muffins are a little more breakfast worthy than corn bread, and a lot more breakfast worthy than pickles. Though, at least if you're Pea Daddy, you could still serve a pickle on the side.

INGREDIENTS

12 paper muffin baking cups, to line muffin tin; or cooking spray or oil, to grease muffin tin

1¼ cups nondairy milk or organic milk

2 tablespoons white vinegar

1½ cups yellow cornmeal

½ cup unbleached all-purpose flour

2 teaspoons baking powder

1 teaspoon salt

¼ cup light brown sugar

2 tablespoons extra-virgin olive oil

¼ cup unsweetened applesauce

1 cup peaches, peeled and diced

2 tablespoons organic sugar

1 teaspoon cinnamon

DIRECTIONS

1 Preheat oven to 375 degrees F. Line a 12-cup muffin tin with paper baking cups or lightly grease with cooking spray or oil and set aside. In a small bowl, combine milk and vinegar. Allow milk mixture to sit for several minutes. This will effectively curdle the milk.

2 Meanwhile, in a large bowl, combine cornmeal, flour, baking powder and salt.

3 Once milk has curdled, mix in brown sugar, oil and applesauce.

4 Pour milk mixture into cornmeal mixture and stir until just combined. Fold in diced peaches.

5 Spoon batter into muffin tin so that each cup is three-quarters full.

6 In a small bowl, mix together sugar and cinnamon. Sprinkle about a teaspoon of cinnamon sugar on each muffin.

7 Bake for 20 to 25 minutes, or until a toothpick inserted in the center of each muffin comes out clean.

NUTRITION INFORMATION PER SERVING: 110 calories, 2 g total fat, 0 g saturated fat, 0 g trans fat, 0 mg cholesterol, 210 mg sodium, 23 g carbohydrate, 2 g fiber, 8 g sugar, 3 g protein, vitamin A 2%, vitamin C 2%, calcium 4%, iron 4%

Cheddar "Bacon" Scones

Makes 10 scones

IT'S BEEN A LONG, LONG TIME SINCE I'VE HAD A MC-ANYTHING.

I don't say that with any degree of superiority. People do what they know. They do what's easy. They do what has nostalgia for them. And while I'm not exactly "lovin' it," I get it.

I have a bit of Mc-nostalgia myself.

I do not miss climbing up into Officer Big Mac's hat in the play area, rung by rung up a dark, cold, unfriendly metal ladder, and peering out the peephole in his custodian helmet, then being terrified to come back down. I do not miss standing in the middle of a barred Grimace, minding my own business, and having some horrible boy come up, taunt me and shake Grimace like crazy, sending my head spinning, while I pleaded for him to stop, tears in my eyes. Stupid brothers. I don't miss mediocre boxes of cookies, burgers with warm pickles and tiny minced onions, which I had to scrape off, and ketchup packets that held enough for two fries. Max.

I do miss sleeping late on Sundays. Waking up with my dad, he in his blue bathrobe and I in my footed pajamas, the smell of coffee in the kitchen and the paper already thumbed through but with the comics left undisturbed for me. My dad would approach us with a piece of paper and a pen in hand, ready to take our order, a big smile on his face, which meant my mom had said he could hit the drive-through for breakfast. It was a rare treat, but it gave my mom a day off from cooking, dishes and being the "bad guy."

I'd never waste my time with the pancakes; Mom made those all the time. And the hash browns were a bit skeevy, with their oblong patty shape wedged in a red cardboard box. I never cared for eggs, so the esteemed McMuffin was out of the question. But, man, did I love those bacon and cheese biscuits. Fluffy dough, melty cheese, crispy, salty bacon. I'd be drooling as I unwrapped the yellow paper and picked the bits of melted cheese off, not wanting to waste a bite.

It's been a long, long time since I've had a Mc-anything.

But I had a cheddar "bacon" scone last Sunday. I ate it in my bathrobe, giddy with nostalgia, picking bits of cheese off the hot pan, not wanting to waste a bite.

I'm not going to single-handedly put the world's biggest fast-food franchise out of business. But there are quick, delicious options out there that are even better than the originals I remember.

INGREDIENTS

cooking spray or oil,
to grease baking sheet

1 cup whole wheat pastry flour

1 cup unbleached all-purpose
flour

1½ tablespoons baking powder

1 teaspoon organic sugar

½ teaspoon salt

⅓ cup vegan margarine
(i.e., Earth Balance) or
organic butter

1 cup nondairy milk
or organic milk

½ cup shredded nondairy
cheddar cheese (i.e., Daiya)
or organic cheddar cheese

1 cup crumbled tempeh bacon
(packaged or from the recipe
on p. 14)

chives, to garnish (optional)

DIRECTIONS

1 Preheat oven to 450 degrees F. Lightly grease a baking sheet with
   cooking spray or oil.

2 In a large bowl, combine flours, baking powder, sugar and salt. Cut
   in vegan margarine or butter a little at a time until the flour mixture
   resembles wet sand. You can also use a food processor for this step,
   pulsing until margarine or butter is incorporated.

3 Pour in milk and stir until just combined. Fold in cheese and bacon.

4 Turn dough out onto a surface that has been lightly floured. Form
   dough into a circle that is approximately 9 inches in diameter and
   about 1½ inches thick. Cut dough into 10 equal wedges. Transfer
   wedges to the baking sheet.

5 Bake scones for 8 to 10 minutes, or until they have set, the bottoms
   are golden brown and the cheese is melty. Garnish with chives,
   if desired.

NUTRITION INFORMATION PER SERVING: 220 calories, 10 g total fat, 30 g saturated fat,
0 g trans fat, 5 mg cholesterol, 350 mg sodium, 25 g carbohydrate, 2 g fiber, 4 g sugar,
7 g protein, vitamin A 2%, vitamin C 0%, calcium 8%, iron 4%

Optional ingredients and toppings not included in analysis.

pea points

You can easily swap
cheese varieties
for a completely
different take on
these scones.
Pepper Jack Daiya
gives a spicy kick to
these scones, or if
you eat real cheese,
smoky Gouda or
Swiss cheese are
a nice change.

more peas, thank you

Creamy Power Porridge

Makes 4 servings of approximately 2 cups each

I DON'T POST MANY BREAKFAST RECIPES ON OUR SITE, BUT IT'S NOT BECAUSE IT'S NOT MY FAVORITE MEAL.

I assure you, breakfast is pretty much the main reason I get up in the morning. Most nights it's the last thing I think of before I go to sleep. I don't dream of waffles or pancakes. I don't wake with a mission for anything complicated or frilly. I usually just want something hearty and hot, creamy and filling. It's something Wilford Brimley and I have in common. I'm not naive enough to think it's the only thing.

I love oatmeal.

And the reason why I am not constantly creating dozens upon dozens of breakfast recipes on our site is that most days oats are all I want. I've graduated from the instant packets, as delicious as I thought they used to be, and I've even moved beyond sticking rolled oats in a pot or the microwave. Our favorite way to eat oats these days is to take hearty, nutty steel-cut oats, grind them finely and then cook them on the stove top with nondairy milk.

But because I like to think of myself as a buff mother, I like to power up my oats with some protein powder, though that truly is optional. What you can't skip, though, are the toppings: berries, nut butter, brown sugar, cinnamon, raisins. The sky's the limit.

I put a pot on when I wake up, find a missing puzzle piece, give the pot a stir, take a shower, give it a stir, throw Gigi's hair up in a sloppy bun, give it a stir, get Lulu a pickle, give it a stir, and voilà! Breakfast is served.

Everyone's a fan and the fact that I can sell it as what Goldilocks eats doesn't hurt, either. More important, it's a breakfast you'll feel proud eating and a breakfast you'll feel proud sending your family out the door with, full in their bellies. It's a breakfast you'll think about before you fall asleep at night.

INGREDIENTS

1 cup steel-cut oats

2 cups nondairy milk
or organic milk

4 cups water, plus 1 cup more
during cooking

1 teaspoon cinnamon

1½ teaspoons nutmeg

stevia, agave or maple syrup
to taste (optional)

4 servings of your favorite
protein powder (look for rice,
pea and/or soy blends)

Toppings:
berries, diced apples, diced
peaches, sliced bananas

dried raisins, cranberries,
apricots

almond butter, sunflower seed
butter, peanut butter

chopped walnuts, pecans
or almonds

DIRECTIONS

1   Grind steel-cut oats in your food processor or high-speed blender.
    The finer you grind them, the creamier your porridge will become.

2   Transfer oats to a large pot and add milk and the 4 cups water.
    Whisk well, beating out any lumps.

3   Bring to a boil over medium-high heat. Lower heat and simmer for
    15 to 18 minutes, stirring every few minutes. If the porridge gets too
    thick, you can add a little more water while cooking and whisk it in
    completely.

4   At the end of the cooking time, add cinnamon, nutmeg, sweetener
    and protein powder (if using) and whisk well to remove any lumps.

5   Transfer porridge to bowls and sprinkle with desired toppings.

NUTRITION INFORMATION PER SERVING: 290 calories, 5 g total fat, 3 g saturated fat,
0 g trans fat, 5 mg cholesterol, 260 mg sodium, 34 g carbohydrate, 4 g fiber, 7 g sugar,
26 g protein, vitamin A 4%, vitamin C 0%, calcium 20%, iron 25%

Optional ingredients and toppings not included in analysis.

more peas, thank you

Easy Apple Oat Cakes

Makes 1 single-serving cake

IF YOU EVER WANT PROOF THAT YOU ARE AN IMPERFECT HUMAN BEING, HAVE CHILDREN.

Because when they don't look you straight in the eye and point out your flaws ("Mom, your hair looks totally weird!"), they leave little reminders.

Like my daughter's toothbrush, sitting nicely on the bathroom counter, filled with toothpaste. It sits there, pristinely untouched, the way you left it. Before she left for preschool ten minutes ago. You walk downstairs and find another reminder. Her toast, now soggy with strawberry jelly, sitting nicely on her purple plastic plate (Lord help you if it's not the purple one). It sits there, pristinely untouched, the way you left it. Before she left for preschool ten minutes ago.

At least there was nothing but funky toddler morning breath to theoretically brush away, and in the grand scheme of things, toddler morning breath is on the low end when it comes to the hierarchy of stank. More proof of your imperfection will rear its ugly head when you call your husband and lash out at him as he drives your innocent, hungry, plaque-y toddler to school.

I don't blame her. Toast is boring.

That's where Easy Apple Oat Cakes come in.

They're easy. They cook in ninety seconds. They're apple. That makes them moist and sweet. They're oats. That makes them healthy. They're cake.

That means there's no way Lulu is willingly leaving for school *without* eating her breakfast. Cake is toddler kryptonite.

Now if there was just a way to work some fluoride and floss into the equation.

INGREDIENTS

1 tablespoon ground flaxseed

2 tablespoons warm water

⅓ cup old-fashioned oats

1 tablespoon chia seeds

1 teaspoon baking powder

stevia to taste

½ teaspoon cinnamon

½ teaspoon nutmeg

pinch of salt

3 tablespoons nondairy milk or organic milk

¼ cup unsweetened applesauce

¼ cup apple, diced

natural peanut or almond butter, nondairy or organic dairy cream cheese or vegan margarine for topping (optional)

cooking spray or oil, to grease bowl

DIRECTIONS

1   In a small bowl, mix together ground flaxseed and water and set aside.

2   In another small bowl, combine oats, chia seeds, baking powder, stevia, cinnamon, nutmeg and salt.

3   After a few minutes, when flaxseed has thickened, add milk and applesauce to it and mix well. Add flaxseed mixture to the oats mixture and stir until just combined. Fold in diced apple.

4   Pour batter into a microwave-safe individual bowl or ramekin that has been lightly greased with cooking spray or oil. Microwave for 90 seconds.

5   Let cake cook slightly before turning out onto a plate or eating straight from the bowl. Top as desired.

pea points

These cakes are also great with blueberries, diced banana or even chocolate chips subbed in for the diced apple.

NUTRITION INFORMATION PER SERVING: 350 calories, 16 g total fat, 3.5 g saturated fat, 0 g trans fat, <5 mg cholesterol, 320 mg sodium, 47 g carbohydrate, 17 g fiber, 12 g sugar, 10 g protein, vitamin A 2%, vitamin C 10%, calcium 25%, iron 25%

Optional ingredients and toppings not included in analysis.

39

Breakfasts

Pineapple Upside-Down Muffins

Makes 6 jumbo muffins
The name says it all—Pineapple Upside-Down Muffins. Only in my house,
we eat it for breakfast!

I HATE TO SHARE.

There, I said it. Revoke my "Mom card." Call *Sesame Street* and my kindergarten teacher. It doesn't matter and it won't change the fact that I want what's mine and you can get your own.

Let me clear this up for you a bit: I had two brothers. Need more? My mom was very frugal. She had to be. We all lived on my dad's salary as a grocery store manager and that meant we often had to do without. Or more specifically, it meant we had to do with half. Fifty percent off is a very good price. But, gosh darn it, sometimes a girl wants her own stick of gum. Her own candy bar. And—dare I dream it?—her very own cake.

The rule in our house was whichever kid splits "it," the other kid gets to choose. This led to multiple fights with my older brother. Upon deciding who was actually going to split, it took a painfully long time to meticulously divide the object of our desire down the exact, mathematical middle, and then came the inevitable fight with my mom as to why she bought the horrible, yet still highly coveted Wrigley's gum. I always seemed to wind up with the littlest chunk of flavorless Doublemint. I would tell myself, *Don't laugh, sneeze or breathe too hard, or you might swallow it*. And you knew my mom wasn't just going to hand over another piece if that happened.

My mom always liked to say, "Wait until you're a mom. You'll see." But the only thing I see is what a pushover I am. Maybe my kids are spoiled. But I just don't want them to end up as little gum-hoarding jerks like me. Maybe that's why I love these muffins so much. You get a tasty, sweet breakfast treat and you get your own.

You heard me right. This one's mine. Get your own.

INGREDIENTS

cooking spray or oil, to grease muffin tin

½ cup organic sugar

1 cup crushed pineapple

½ cup pineapple juice

⅔ cup whole wheat pastry flour

⅔ cup unbleached all-purpose flour

1 tablespoon baking powder

½ teaspoon salt

Pineapple topping:
2 tablespoons vegan margarine (i.e., Earth Balance), coconut oil or organic butter

¼ cup light brown sugar

6 pineapple rings

6 fresh raspberries or cherries

DIRECTIONS

1   Preheat oven to 350 degrees F. Lightly grease a 6-cup, jumbo-size muffin tin with cooking spray or oil.

2   In a blender, combine sugar, crushed pineapple and pineapple juice. Cover and blend until smooth.

3   In a large bowl, combine flours, baking powder and salt. Pour pineapple mixture into dry ingredients and stir until moistened.

4   In a small saucepan, melt margarine or coconut oil or butter and brown sugar over low heat. Cook for one minute.

5   Place a pineapple ring in the center of each muffin cup. Spoon an equal amount of the brown sugar mixture over each pineapple ring. Fill each cup three-quarters full with muffin batter.

6   Bake muffins for 20 to 25 minutes, or until they have set.

7   Allow muffins to cool in the tin for 3 minutes. Run a knife around the edge of each muffin to loosen. Place a wire cooling rack over the muffin tin and then quickly flip it over to release muffins.

8   Garnish with raspberries or cherries.

NUTRITION INFORMATION PER SERVING: 290 calories, 4 g total fat, 1 g saturated fat, 0 g trans fat, 0 mg cholesterol, 380 mg sodium, 61 g carbohydrate, 3 g fiber, 39 g sugar, 3 g protein, vitamin A 0%, vitamin C 15%, calcium 2%, iron 6%

41

Breakfasts

Pineapple Upside-Down Muffins

Maple Apple Spice Coffee Cake

Maple Apple Spice Coffee Cake

Makes 9 servings

I'M NOT GOING TO SUGGEST YOU SHOULD EAT CAKE FOR BREAKFAST EVERY MORNING.

But this coffee cake is incredible for entertaining at a weekend brunch or for noshing on a holiday morning, while rummaging through stockings. I've added a little twist to the Apple Spice Coffee Cake that's previously appeared on our website: a sweet maple glaze that puts it over the top. Not to say that the original was without its fans.

My favorite surprise was when we went out to eat at our favorite local restaurant, Venti's Cafe, and the owner's nephew, Conrad, came up and said, "Hi, Peas!" I had no idea he was a reader, and then he said, "My kids love your Apple Spice Coffee Cake! We make it almost every weekend."

There's no coffee cake on Venti's menu. But there just might be someday, and if there is, I'll bet it's this one.

INGREDIENTS

Cake:
cooking spray or oil,
to grease baking pan

½ cup nondairy milk

¾ cup unsweetened applesauce

¼ cup extra-virgin olive oil or melted coconut oil

1 teaspoon vanilla extract

½ cup organic light brown sugar

1 cup whole wheat pastry flour

1 cup oat flour

1½ teaspoons baking powder

½ teaspoon baking soda

1 teaspoon cinnamon

½ teaspoon nutmeg

½ teaspoon salt

1 medium apple, peeled, cored and diced

Streusel topping:
3 tablespoons organic light brown sugar

1 tablespoon organic sugar

3 tablespoons whole wheat pastry flour

2½ tablespoons vegan margarine (i.e., Earth Balance) or organic butter

¼ cup old-fashioned oats

2 teaspoons cinnamon

Maple glaze:
¼ cup nondairy or organic cream cheese

1½ cups organic powdered sugar

½ teaspoon maple extract

pinch of salt

1 to 2 tablespoons maple syrup

DIRECTIONS

1 Preheat oven to 350 degrees F. Lightly grease an 8 x 8-inch baking pan with cooking spray or oil.

2 In a small mixing bowl or a large liquid measuring cup, combine milk, applesauce, oil, vanilla and brown sugar.

3 In a large bowl, combine flours, baking powder, baking soda, cinnamon, nutmeg and salt.

4 Add applesauce mixture to flour mixture and stir until just combined. Add diced apple to batter and fold in gently.

5 Spoon batter into the 8 x 8-inch baking pan.

6 In a small bowl, mix together all the streusel topping ingredients until the topping is uniform in consistency. Sprinkle topping evenly over the top of the batter.

7 Bake for 28 to 32 minutes, or until a toothpick inserted in the center comes out clean.

8 To prepare maple glaze, beat together cream cheese, powdered sugar, maple extract and salt in a medium bowl with a handheld mixer. Add as much maple syrup as necessary to make glaze pourable. Drizzle glaze over the top of the cake.

9 Cut cake into squares and serve.

NUTRITION INFORMATION PER SERVING: 420 calories, 13 g total fat, 2.5 g saturated fat, 0 g trans fat, 0 mg cholesterol, 290 mg sodium, 76 g carbohydrate, 5 g fiber, 48 g sugar, 4 g protein, vitamin A 0%, vitamin C 2%, calcium 2%, iron 6%

Pumpkin Cinnamon Rolls

Makes 6 large rolls

"IN THE BEGINNING, MAMA CREATED CINNAMON ROLLS. AND THEY WERE GOOD."

It's quite fitting that these cinnamon rolls are the last recipe in this chapter. These delicious, decadent sweet rolls are one of the first recipes I ever posted on my blog, way back in November of 2010. Who knew then that anyone would ever cook a single thing I posted? I was just too lazy to buy a recipe box.

Ah, how much has changed since then. My babies are getting older. My hair is getting grayer. And I never did buy that recipe box. But one thing that hasn't changed is how much everyone clamors for these cinnamon rolls. As reader Linzi said, "These are. To. Die. For. I have a new Christmas morning tradition."

Hope you'll add these to your Christmas morning tradition, as well. Or at least to your recipe box.

INGREDIENTS

1 packet active dry yeast

¼ cup sugar

1 cup nondairy milk or organic milk, warmed to between 105 and 115 degrees F

2 cups whole wheat pastry flour

½ cup organic unbleached all-purpose flour

½ teaspoon cinnamon

½ teaspoon nutmeg

¼ teaspoon salt

1 tablespoon baking powder

¼ cup canned pumpkin

Filling:

½ cup organic light brown sugar

1 tablespoon cinnamon

2 tablespoons vegan margarine (i.e., Earth Balance) or organic butter, softened

2 tablespoons raisins (optional)

cooking spray, to grease baking pan

Icing:

1 cup powdered sugar

½ teaspoon vanilla extract

pinch of salt

1 to 2 tablespoons nondairy milk or organic milk

DIRECTIONS

1 In a medium bowl, dissolve yeast and sugar in warm milk. Set aside and allow yeast to activate for 5 to 8 minutes, or until foamy.

2 Combine flours, cinnamon, nutmeg, salt and baking powder in a large bowl. In a small bowl, prepare the filling by combining brown sugar, cinnamon and margarine or butter.

3 Once yeast mixture is foamy, stir in pumpkin. Add pumpkin mixture to flour mixture and stir gently until a dough forms.

4 Turn dough out onto floured work surface and knead for a minute or so (about 20 times). Knead in as much extra flour (up to ¼ cup) as necessary so that dough is no longer sticky.

5 Roll dough into a large rectangle. Sprinkle filling over dough. Top with raisins, if using. Roll dough up firmly to make a log.

6 Cut the log into six equal pieces and place in a loaf pan or 8 x 8-inch baking pan that has been greased with cooking spray.

7 Cover rolls loosely with a tea towel and let them rise in a warm place for at least 40 minutes. Or the rolls can be covered and refrigerated overnight.

8 Preheat oven to 350 degrees F. Bake rolls for 23 to 25 minutes, or until golden brown.

9 Prepare the icing by stirring together powdered sugar, vanilla and salt. Add as much milk as necessary to reach a smooth, drizzling consistency.

10 Drizzle cooled rolls with icing.

46

NUTRITION INFORMATION PER SERVING: 440 calories, 4.5 g total fat, 1.5 g saturated fat, 0 g trans fat, <5 mg cholesterol, 250 mg sodium, 94 g carbohydrate, 7 g fiber, 51 g sugar, 7 g protein, vitamin A 25%, vitamin C 0%, calcium 8%, iron 8%

Optional ingredients and toppings not included in analysis.

more peas, thank you

Snacks, Sides
and Sauces

Ranch Kale Chips 50

Balsamic Roasted
Brussels Sprouts 52

Pizza Popcorn 55

Ranch Dressing 58

Curry Roasted Sweet
Potatoes 60

Green Bean Fries 62

Chocolate Peanut
Butter Protein Truffles 63

Chocolate Cherry
Cashew Bars 65

Almond Raisin Biscotti 69

Cranberry Blueberry
Sauce 71

Coconut Rice 73

Sweet Potato Dream 76

Carrot Orange Pistachio
Streusel Muffins 79

Mmmm Sauces 83

Salsa Verde 90

Better Bay Biscuits 92

Quinoa Tabouleh 94

Almost Chipotle
Guacamole 96

Cracklin' Cauliflower 97

Ranch Kale Chips

Makes 2 large or 4 small servings

I CAN'T LIE TO YOU.

My kids, yes, I lie to them daily. Okay, hourly. So what if I'm not really super, super excited because you put your shirt on by yourself, if I didn't count out the number of blueberries on your yogurt to make sure you have the exact same amount as your sister, and if Dad really isn't dying to read you *If You Give a Mouse a Cookie* for the thirty-seventh time when he gets home? Sorry, honey. As far as the girls are concerned, these are all universal truths.

But I can't lie to you.

Kale chips are not potato chips. They don't taste a thing like potato chips. Sure, they are crispy and go well with a sandwich, but they aren't potato chips. Kale chips will not scoop up onion dip every day of your nine months of pregnancy. That was me with Gigi. Onion dip and root beer floats. I was eating for two, which I sometimes got confused with twenty-two. Kale chips don't come in a can that has a magnetic pull, that sucks your hand inside like it's a vacuum hose, and you certainly won't dump a can of kale chips upside down on your face to get every last crumb. That was me again.

But, on the bright side, kale chips, unlike potato chips, do not look so much like fingernail clippings that you might find a "chip" on the couch, pop it in your mouth and then realize mid-chew that it is not in fact a chip. That was my mom. Sorry, Mom. Aren't you glad I became a writer?

If that story in and of itself doesn't convince you to swap your potato chips for kale chips, I don't know what will. Except maybe ranch-flavored kale chips. They are not potato chips, but they are awesome. And that's no lie.

INGREDIENTS

cooking spray or oil, to grease baking sheet

1 bunch of kale, de-stemmed and cut into bite-size pieces

1 lemon, juiced

1 teaspoon garlic powder

1 teaspoon onion powder

¼ teaspoon dry mustard

¼ teaspoon dried dill

1 teaspoon dried parsley

1 teaspoon salt

DIRECTIONS

1 Preheat oven to 300 degrees F. Prepare a baking sheet by lightly greasing with cooking spray or oil.

2 Spread kale pieces evenly on the baking sheet. Squeeze lemon juice over the kale.

3 In a small bowl, combine garlic powder, onion powder, mustard, dill, parsley and salt.

4 Sprinkle spice blend over the top of the kale.

5 Bake kale for 20 to 25 minutes, turning every ten minutes or so. Watch kale carefully toward the end of the baking time as it will burn if left unattended. Chips should be crisp and light. Serve them immediately.

pea points

If ranch isn't your thing, omit the spice blend and just top the kale with salt. You'll still have some mighty tasty chips on your hands.

Snacks, Sides and Sauces

NUTRITION INFORMATION PER SERVING: 40 calories, 1.5 g total fat, 0 g saturated fat, 0 g trans fat, 0 mg cholesterol, 620 mg sodium, 6 g carbohydrate, 1 g fiber, <1 g sugar, 2 g protein, vitamin A 30%, vitamin C 120%, calcium 10%, iron 8%

Based on 4 servings.

Balsamic Roasted Brussels Sprouts

Makes 4 servings of approximately ¾ cup each

THERE ARE TWO THINGS I'M IN CHARGE OF EVERY HOLIDAY IN MY FAMILY—THE PIES AND THE BRUSSELS SPROUTS.

I'm in charge of the pies because no one else wants to do it, and I'm in charge of the brussels sprouts because no one else wants to eat them. That is totally fine by me, though. I love brussels sprouts.

So even though I could sell ice to Eskimos, or tofu to husbands, as the case may be, I don't try to persuade the masses to eat brussels sprouts on Thanksgiving or Easter. In fact, I do just the opposite and play up all the other side dishes.

"Mom, these are the best sweet potatoes you've ever made."

"Aunt Manya, seriously, next year you should make more rolls, because those are going fast!"

"Dad, that stuffing? I want to wash my face with it, put some behind my ears and on the nape of my neck, and then take off my shoes and soak my feet in it. And I'm going to, so everybody better fill their plates. Now."

And then I try to downplay the sprouts as much as I can. If anyone asks me how they are, I simply say, "I guess they're okay, if you like sprouts."

Since nobody does, I get the whole bowl to myself.

Go ahead, make this recipe and then don't hype the sprouts up to your family. Tell them they aren't great. Give them the hard sell on the cranberries and the green beans. And then save all the sprouts for yourself. Just keep your shoes on.

more peas, thank you

INGREDIENTS

2 tablespoons good quality olive oil or vegan margarine (i.e., Earth Balance)

3 cups brussels sprouts, trimmed and halved

¼ cup balsamic vinegar

2 teaspoons light brown sugar

salt and pepper to taste

DIRECTIONS

1 Preheat oven to 400 degrees F.

2 Heat oil or margarine in an oven-safe sauté pan or a cast-iron skillet. Put sprouts in skillet, cut side down, and cook without turning or moving until undersides are browned and crusted, approximately 4 to 5 minutes.

3 Transfer pan to oven and roast for 4 minutes.

4 In a small liquid measuring cup, combine vinegar and brown sugar.

5 Remove pan from oven and flip each sprout over. Pour vinegar mixture over sprouts, swirling vinegar mixture around the pan to remove any loose bits.

6 Season with salt and pepper and serve immediately. To yourself.

NUTRITION INFORMATION PER SERVING: 100 calories, 6 g total fat, 1.5 g saturated fat, 0 g trans fat, 0 mg cholesterol, 65 mg sodium, 10 g carbohydrate, 3 g fiber, 6 g sugar, 2 g protein, vitamin A 10%, vitamin C 90%, calcium 2%, iron 6%

more peas, thank you

Pizza Popcorn

Makes 5 servings of 2 cups each

WE ARE INTO THEME PARTIES IN OUR HOUSE.

This, of course, is just another trait we have in common with a frat house, along with frequently spilled drinks and people without pants.

Each year, when a birthday is looming, we run through a long list of possible themes for the birthday girl's (or boy's) party. I'd be lying if I said that I didn't take into serious consideration how hard or easy it would be to make a relevant cake. I bought a cake pan shaped like a very non-specific animal face and it has been a cat, a bear and Dora. Sorry, Dora.

A few unique themes have popped up occasionally as options, but I shoot those down as fast as I can. The pony party with live ponies wasn't happening. Neither was the Sanjaya party. Yes, *that* Sanjaya, from *American Idol*. Where a two-year-old Gigi got the idea to have a Sanjaya party, I don't know, but there was no way I was going to make a Sanjaya cake. So we went with unicorns and butterflies.

As Lulu's fourth birthday edged closer and closer, we had no doubt what theme she would choose. If it wasn't the eighteen stuffed dogs on her bed that gave her away, it was when she somehow found a way to access our blog via my iPhone, created a new document and published the one-word post, aptly titled "Dog." She got ninety-seven comments.

A puppy party I could do. I had the perfect cake pan for it. I had paw print cupcakes, stick pretzels to play fetch with, puppy games and crafts, and this delicious pizza-flavored snack that disappeared faster than Sanjaya: pizza pupcorn.

After the party, when all our guests had left with their puppy goody bags and the last pupcorn kernel had been eaten, I gave the birthday girl a big hug.

"I love you more than ice cream!" I told Lulu.

"I love you more than presents!" she told me back.

"I love you more than cake!" I continued.

She thought, put her finger to her lips and thought some more.

"I love puppies more than you!" she announced.

It's okay. I totally expected that.

INGREDIENTS

parchment paper, to line large
baking sheet

¼ cup vegan margarine (i.e.,
Earth Balance) or organic butter
or extra-virgin olive oil

⅓ cup nutritional yeast or
parmesan cheese

1 teaspoon salt

½ teaspoon garlic powder

¼ teaspoon onion powder

½ teaspoon dried oregano

½ teaspoon dried basil

10 cups air-popped popcorn

DIRECTIONS

1   Preheat oven to 350 degrees F. Line a large baking sheet with
    parchment paper for easy cleanup.

2   In a small saucepan, melt margarine or butter, if using, or gently
    heat olive oil. Add nutritional yeast, salt, garlic powder, onion
    powder, oregano and basil.

3   Spread popcorn on the baking sheet. Pour spice mixture over
    popcorn and toss to coat.

4   Bake for 15 to 20 minutes, tossing popcorn at least once
    during baking.

NUTRITION INFORMATION PER SERVING: 180 calories, 10 g total fat, 2.5 saturated fat,
0 g trans fat, 0 mg cholesterol, 550 mg sodium, 17 g carbohydrate, 5 g fiber, 0 g sugar,
7 g protein, vitamin A 2%, vitamin C 0%, calcium 2%, iron 6%

Ranch Dressing

Makes 2 cups (sixteen 2 tablespoon servings)
Dare I suggest that this recipe is as good as the ranch from the secluded place between two mountains? Yes, I dare.

MISTAKES I MADE IN MIDDLE SCHOOL:

1 Intentionally wearing the exact same outfit as my best friend on the first day of school. Liz never wore that outfit again. I wore it at least twice a week.

2 Math team.

3 Not getting the nerve up to ask my mom if I could start shaving until after volleyball day in gym class. In a tank top. When *Harry and the Hendersons* was number one at the box office.

4 Green eyeliner.

5 Trying out for the lead in the school play so that my first kiss will forever be a) fake; and b) with an eighth-grader named Jon, who already had lots of practice in the halls with his "experienced" girlfriend. I was so very afraid of her. And Jon's mouth.

6 Wearing my grandma's hand-me-down loafers.

7 Giving the wrong answer in front of the class in pre-algebra, shrugging and telling the teacher, "I guess I screwed the pooch this time!"

8 Getting kicked off the math team.

9 Not realizing, while watching all my friends flirt shamelessly with my older brother when they'd come over, that maybe I wasn't winning people over with my sparkling personality.

10 Aqua Net + curling iron + comb + more Aqua Net.

11 Taking advantage of the cafeteria's all-you-can-pump ranch dressing on French fries, Tater Tots, pizza, burgers, grilled cheese, packed-from-home bologna sandwiches and potato chips. In my tapestry vest, green eyeliner, Grandma's loafers and mall bangs. And then going to drama practice for kissing. Sorry, Jon.

INGREDIENTS

¾ cup nondairy milk (unsweetened, unflavored) or organic milk

½ cup extra-virgin olive oil

½ cup water

1 tablespoon apple cider vinegar

2 teaspoons lemon juice

1 teaspoon garlic powder

1 teaspoon onion powder

1 teaspoon salt

¼ teaspoon dried dill

¼ teaspoon ground mustard

2 teaspoons fresh parsley, minced

freshly ground black pepper to taste

DIRECTIONS

1 Combine all ingredients in a blender or shaker bottle and blend or shake until combined.

2 Store in an airtight container in the fridge for up to two weeks.

NUTRITION INFORMATION PER SERVING: 70 calories, 7 g total fat, 1 g saturated fat, 0 g trans fat, 0 mg cholesterol, 150 mg sodium, <1 g carbohydrate, 0 g fiber, 0 g sugar, 0 g protein, vitamin A 0%, vitamin C 0%, calcium 2%, iron 2%

Based on 16 servings of 2 tablespoons each.

Curry Roasted Sweet Potatoes

Makes 4 servings

MY KIDS ARE CRAZY.

It has nothing to do with the fact that they each gave up naps at a little over a year old, meaning that there were at least fourteen waking hours of tea parties, ballet "recitals," dress up and *Calliou* episodes each day. That has more to do with why I am crazy.

It has nothing to do with the fearless way they burst into a meticulously choreographed two-person flash mob of Katy Perry's "Firework" on the frozen food aisle, complete with those cursed mini-carts as props. That has more to do with why I am crazy. And have bruised ankles.

I base my children's crazy diagnosis on the fact that neither one of them likes sweet potatoes. Fine by me. That just means there are more for me and Pea Daddy, and I can make them as spicy as I like them.

And these Curry Roasted Sweet Potatoes? Well, they're just crazy good.

INGREDIENTS

2 teaspoons curry powder

¾ teaspoon ground ginger

½ teaspoon cinnamon

½ teaspoon garam masala

1 teaspoon organic sugar or stevia equivalent

½ teaspoon sea salt

2 tablespoons nondairy milk or organic milk

1 teaspoon lemon juice

1 pound sweet potatoes, cut into large wedges

cooking spray, to grease baking sheet

DIRECTIONS

1 Preheat oven to 425 degrees F.

2 In a large bowl, combine curry powder, ginger, cinnamon, garam masala, sweetener, salt, milk and lemon juice. Add sweet potatoes and toss to coat.

3 Place potatoes on a baking sheet that has been greased with cooking spray. Bake for 23 to 25 minutes, or until crisp, turning at least once during the baking time.

NUTRITION INFORMATION PER SERVING: 110 calories, 0 g total fat, 0 g saturated fat, 0 g trans fat, 0 mg cholesterol, 590 mg sodium, 26 g carbohydrate, 4 g fiber, 6 g sugar, 2 g protein, vitamin A 320%, vitamin C 4%, calcium 4%, iron 4%

Green Bean Fries

Makes 4 servings

I FEEL A LITTLE FUNNY CALLING THIS A RECIPE, BUT SOMETIMES THE BEST THINGS IN LIFE ARE THE SIMPLEST.

A little child reaching up and grabbing your hand (after they've just washed their hands). A little child patting you on the cheek and saying "Good morning" (after they've just washed their hands). A little child going in the bathroom completely on their own, using the potty (and then, you guessed it, washing their hands).

Miracles happen. Simple, totally hygienic miracles.

These "fries" have my girls begging to eat green beans on almost a daily basis. And better still, they get to use their hands. Their very, very clean hands.

Amen.

INGREDIENTS

1 pound green beans, ends trimmed

1 tablespoon extra-virgin olive oil

1 teaspoon sea salt

DIRECTIONS

1   Preheat oven to 425 degrees F.

2   Toss green beans with olive oil and salt.

3   Spread green beans on a baking sheet. Roast for 12 to 14 minutes, turning at least once during cooking, or until beans are crisp and just starting to brown.

NUTRITION INFORMATION PER SERVING: 60 calories, 3.5 g total fat, 0 g saturated fat, 0 g trans fat, 0 mg cholesterol, 580 mg sodium, 8 g carbohydrate, 4 g fiber, 2 g sugar, 2 g protein, vitamin A 15%, vitamin C 30%, calcium 4%, iron 6%

pea points

I love to dip these fries in ketchup, but they're also great with the ranch dressing (p. 58) and any of the Mmmm Sauces (p. 83).

more peas, thank you

Chocolate Peanut Butter Protein Truffles

Makes 10 truffles

THERE'S A COMMON MYTH WHEN IT COMES TO EATING A MEATLESS DIET, AND THAT MYTH HAS TO DO WITH PROTEIN.

Another common myth has to do with beans and their musicality. That one is unfortunately very true and the reason why we really, really enjoy scented candles in our house. Almost daily, though, I'm asked, "Where do you get your protein?" And though I am not a nutritionist or a doctor and am far better at giving hugs, cookies and French braids than medical advice, I have two answers that I've picked up along the way.

One answer is that as Americans, we actually have a surplus of protein in our diet, and research shows that if you have enough calories in your diet, you will have enough protein. The problem I have with that answer, though, is that I, my friends, am allergic to sleeves. And I like lifting weights, sculpting my arms and then showing up wearing a tank top at completely inappropriate times. We all have our issues. But such a habit requires a little extra protein, especially after a workout.

Which leads to my second answer to the "Where do you get your protein?" question. That answer is truffles. I like to do some bicep curls and then eat chocolate. It works.

Welcome to the gun show. Light a candle on your way out.

INGREDIENTS

½ cup old-fashioned oats or oat flour

⅓ cup protein powder (vanilla or chocolate)

⅓ cup ground flaxseed

3 tablespoons cocoa powder

¼ cup natural peanut butter

½ teaspoon vanilla extract

¼ to ½ cup water

dash of salt

stevia to taste

If using old-fashioned oats, grind them into a flour in a blender or food processor.

DIRECTIONS

1   In a large bowl, combine oat flour, protein powder, ground flaxseed and cocoa powder. Stir in peanut butter, vanilla and enough water to make a dough. Add salt and adjust stevia to taste.

2   Using a large spoon, scoop mixture and shape into Ping-Pong-size balls. Roll until smooth.

3   Chill for 30 minutes to allow truffles to set.

pea points

Try different nut butters to switch things up. Almond butter is phenomenal and sunflower seed butter is great for those with nut allergies.

NUTRITION INFORMATION PER SERVING: 90 calories, 4 g total fat, 1 g saturated fat, 0 g trans fat, 15 mg cholesterol, 65 mg sodium, 5 g carbohydrate, 1 g fiber, <1 g sugar, 8 g protein, vitamin A 10%, vitamin C 10%, calcium 4%, iron 15%

more peas, thank you

Chocolate Cherry Cashew Bars

Makes 12 bars

These bars are similar to a certain *kind* of chocolate cherry bar you can find at many *kinds* of grocery and natural foods stores.

PEA DADDY IS SUCH A DIPLOMAT.

We've been talking a bit about our finances lately, trying to figure out the best way to set money aside for both the girls for college, pay off our school loans and really be wise with our choices. I have to admit, I've gotten a little lazy when it comes to the "being wise with our choices" part. I blame changing seasons, seasonal flavors and sweater season. Curse you, Fall.

Enter Mr. Subtle.

Recently Pea Daddy, in between suggested Groupon and LivingSocial deals he wanted me to buy, sent me an email with a link to an article entitled "The Only 2 Financial Rules You Need to Live By."

The rules are:

1 Pay yourself first (in savings and retirement, not Pumpkin Spice Lattes); and

2 Practice mindful spending (not buying every shade of boyfriend cardigan available).

My very careful husband than added after the link his own personal admission, "*I* know *I've* gotten really bad at rule number 2." Translation: *You,* dear wife, have gotten really bad at rule number 2.

So I came up with a list of some of the ways we can save money as a household. I started packing Pea Daddy's lunch, every day, in my old lululemon bags, not in a *Star Wars* lunchbox as he'd requested. I started drinking tap water instead of fruity bottled water. I had been watering down my bottled drinks by about 50 percent, patting myself on the back because it wasn't vodka. But still, I could do better.

I started making coffee drinks at home. I failed miserably at giving up coffee altogether. But that doesn't mean the next book should be sponsored by Starbucks. (Psst, Starbucks. Call me.) I started making our own snack bars. I rely on bars when we're on the go, and packaged bars are not good for my wallet. Or my marriage. "Got enough bars?" Pea Daddy likes to ask as I add twelve to our grocery cart.

Nope.

So here's one more. But as soon as I make these, I always pay myself first.

INGREDIENTS

parchment paper, to line baking sheet

3 tablespoons ground flaxseeds (or approximately 2 tablespoons whole flaxseeds before grinding)

½ cup maple syrup or honey (or a mixture of the two)

1 teaspoon salt

1 cup whole almonds, coarsely chopped

½ cup peanuts, coarsely chopped

½ cup cashew pieces

½ cup dried cherries

½ cup semisweet chocolate chips

DIRECTIONS

1 Preheat oven to 350 degrees F. Line an 8 x 8-inch baking sheet with parchment paper.

2 In a small bowl, combine ground flaxseed and sweetener. Mix well and set aside.

3 In a large bowl, combine salt, almonds, peanuts, cashews and cherries. Pour flaxseed-syrup mixture over nuts and cherries and stir until evenly coated.

4 Spread the nut mixture on the baking sheet evenly, from corner to corner.

5 Bake for approximately 25 minutes, or until nuts are slightly brown and edges are crisp. The nut layer will be soft but will harden upon cooling.

6 Melt chocolate chips in a small bowl in the microwave or over a double boiler. Drizzle chocolate over almost cooled nut layer. Chocolate will be wet but will set upon cooling.

7 When nut layer and chocolate have set, pull parchment paper from baking sheet and set bars on a flat cutting surface. Cut nut layer into twelve equal squares, and store in an airtight container. Bars will stay especially crunchy if you refrigerate them.

NUTRITION INFORMATION PER SERVING: 210 calories, 12 g total fat, 2.5 g saturated fat, 0 g trans fat, <5 mg cholesterol, 200 mg sodium, 23 g carbohydrate, 3 g fiber, 17 g sugar, 5 g protein, vitamin A 0%, vitamin C 0%, calcium 4%, iron 6%

Snacks, Sides and Sauces

Almond Raisin Biscotti

Makes 24 to 30 cookies

These biscotti are reminiscent of those store-bought almond raisin cookies I enjoyed during those late-night feedings. You don't need a baby to enjoy these babies, though.

YOU KNOW HOW SOME THINGS YOU SAY ARE JUST SO INCREDULOUS, YOU FEAR SAYING THEM OUT LOUD?

Well, here goes. I kind of miss breast-feeding.

Mind you, for a full year of Gigi's life and eighteen months (that's right, *eighteen months*) of Lulu's, I was counting down the days until they were weaned. Of course it was a bonding experience, and as they say, a type of closeness I'll never know again. But more than that it was exhausting and often felt like an unfair burden, seeing that neither girl would even consider a bottle. As a result, I nursed those girls everywhere. On airplanes, on a beach in Hawaii, in the restroom underneath Space Mountain at Disneyland. And finally, when I had no choice but to wean Lulu when I blew out my back and, thanks to medication, was no longer a functioning member of this world or any other, I was a bit relieved.

So what in the world could I miss? Well, the closeness, which I may never again experience. And the snacks. Every decent book about breast-feeding will tell you to make the nursing session enjoyable for yourself by turning on soothing music and enjoying a snack. For me, that meant Food Network and cookies. Hallelujah, amen. But it wasn't just any cookie. There were these amazing almond raisin cookies that I just loved. There was something about the crunchy nuts and the chewy raisins in these little guys that made being up in the middle of the night with a crying baby and Guy Fieri that much better. I would grab a cup of tea or warm almond milk and a few of these cookies and suddenly didn't mind 3:00 a.m. so much anymore.

I don't know if I'll ever get to experience breast-feeding again. It may not be in the cards. But even if I don't, the next time I make these biscotti, I may just set my alarm and try one with an episode of *Diners, Drive-Ins and Dives.* You know, just for old times' sake.

69

Or I'll just eat one straight from the pan and sleep right through the night. Yeah, that's more like it.

INGREDIENTS

parchment paper, to line baking sheet; or baking spray or oil, to grease baking sheet

1 cup unbleached all-purpose flour

½ cup whole wheat pastry flour

⅔ cup sugar

1 tablespoon cornmeal

1 teaspoon baking powder

½ teaspoon salt

¼ teaspoon aniseed

½ teaspoon cinnamon

¼ cup vegan margarine (i.e., Earth Balance) or coconut oil

⅓ cup unsweetened applesauce

⅔ cup roasted almonds, chopped

¼ cup raisins

DIRECTIONS

1 Preheat oven to 325 degrees F. Line a baking sheet with parchment paper or grease it with baking spray or oil.

2 In a large bowl, combine flours, sugar, cornmeal, baking powder, salt, aniseed and cinnamon. Cut in margarine or add coconut oil, or add flour mixture and margarine to a food processor and pulse until incorporated.

3 Stir in applesauce until a dough forms. Fold in almonds and raisins.

4 Shape dough into a log and place on the baking sheet.

5 Bake for approximately 30 minutes, or until log is firm and has started to brown. Allow log to cool for several minutes and then slice on the diagonal to make cookies that are approximately ½-inch thick.

6 Gently place cookies on one cut side on the baking sheet and bake for 5 minutes. Remove from oven, flip cookies onto their other side, and bake another 5 minutes. Store in an airtight container.

NUTRITION INFORMATION PER SERVING: 80 calories, 3 g total fat, 0.5 g saturated fat, 0 g trans fat, 0 mg cholesterol, 65 mg sodium, 11 g carbohydrate, <1 g fiber, 6 g sugar, 1 g protein, vitamin A 0%, vitamin C 0%, calcium 4%, iron 2%

Based on 30 cookies.

Cranberry Blueberry Sauce

Makes approximately 3 cups

CRANBERRY SAUCE IS ONE OF THOSE THINGS WITH WHICH YOU SHOULD NEVER TAKE THE EASY WAY OUT. NEVER.

Cranberry sauce is like a greeting card. You could go to Hallmark and easily shell out $4.95. Someone works very hard to write those cards. With any luck, you might even find a card that says exactly how you feel, one that plays "Macarena," one that has a picture of a Chihuahua wearing a bathrobe, curlers and lipstick. You might find a card that has all those amazing features in one amazing spectacle, and you might think it is just the right thing to bring a smile to someone special's face. It's not. Don't buy that card. I'm begging you.

Because, you see, even if you think you've found the perfect greeting card, it doesn't come close to a homemade card. Or, at the least, a very heartfelt message written inside a very basic card. That doesn't light up. Or play nineties Top 40 hits. Or have pets wearing people clothes.

Same goes for cranberry sauce. Sure, you could buy a can. Someone hardly puts in any effort at all to make that sauce. If you buy the whole-berry style, you are bordering on forgivable. But if you buy the kind that stays in the shape of the container it comes in, that farts as it slides out of the can and that you have to slice? I don't think we can be friends.

The one and only problem with homemade cranberry sauce is that you usually have to add a whole lot of sugar to cut the sour. In a momentary glimpse of brilliance, I decided to add some sweet blueberries to my homemade sauce one year. It's like a symphony. Not a mariachi band.

Everyone in my family knows I give the best cards. My goal is to make every single person tear up with every single card I give them. I have 100 percent accuracy.

Everyone in my family knows I make the best cranberry sauce. And if you make this sauce, your family will too.

Forget the can. Make this sauce. Let's be friends.

INGREDIENTS

1 12-ounce package
fresh cranberries

1 cup orange juice

½ cup organic sugar

1 teaspoon cinnamon

½ teaspoon nutmeg

1 cup blueberries

DIRECTIONS

1 Rinse and drain cranberries and set aside.

2 Bring orange juice and sugar to a boil in a medium saucepan over medium-high heat. Add cranberries, reduce heat and simmer for about 10 minutes, or until cranberries have burst and sauce has slightly thickened.

3 Stir in cinnamon and nutmeg and remove from heat.

4 Stir in blueberries, smashing a few as you go.

5 Transfer to a serving dish and allow to cool.

NUTRITION INFORMATION PER SERVING: 30 calories, 0 g total fat, 0 g saturated fat, 0 g trans fat, 0 mg cholesterol, 0 mg sodium, 8 g carbohydrate, <1 g fiber, 6 g sugar, 0 g protein, vitamin A 0%, vitamin C 15%, calcium 0%, iron 0%

Based on 24 servings of 2 tablespoons each.

pea points

If you are making this for Thanksgiving dinner, double your batch and freeze half for Christmas. It's not that far away and you'll want some of this sauce on your holiday table.

more peas, thank you

Coconut Rice

Makes 8 servings of approximately ½ cup each

IF YOU THINK I WAS BORN KNOWING HOW TO COOK, YOU THOUGHT WRONG.

And you obviously aren't married to me. When Pea Daddy met me, I knew how to cook two things. The first? Chicken and rice. The second? Rice and chicken.

I wasn't working too hard to impress him, either, because he knew darn well if he was coming over for dinner, he was getting a heaping bowl of sticky rice with a hefty serving of overcooked chicken. Perhaps this is why whenever he showed up at my door for dinner, he always had a Jamba Juice in one hand. And another Jamba Juice in the other hand. For me. And then I knew I wanted to have his babies.

I could never get the chicken quite right. But the rice? I always got the rice spot-on. That was due to a little friend of mine called the rice cooker. What a strange and brilliant invention! You popped in the rice, you popped in the water, and in what seemed like an eternity, you got a perfectly cooked batch of rice, a super sticky pot to clean, starchy, steamy water all over your cupboards and yet another appliance to store. Still, it was easy, and thus I carbo-loaded my way through law school on a steady diet of rice, rice and more rice.

I still have my rice cooker somewhere, tucked away with a waffle iron, an ice cream maker with a broken paddle and the juicer that gets invited in for weeks at a time, only to be excommunicated soon thereafter, when I remember how much I like to chew. Because, you see, I've learned how to cook rice and cook it well. I even know how to do it in a pot. On the stove. In a respectable amount of time.

When I tell Pea Daddy we are having coconut rice with dinner, he hurries home. Something tells me from the way he heaps his plate, he's not stopping for a smoothie on the way. Or at least he's hiding the proof in the trash.

INGREDIENTS

1 tablespoon coconut oil, vegan margarine (i.e., Earth Balance) or organic butter

1 tablespoon light brown sugar

½ teaspoon salt

½ teaspoon ground ginger

2 cups brown jasmine rice

1 15-ounce can coconut milk (full or reduced fat)

⅓ cup water

¼ cup unsweetened coconut, toasted

chopped scallions and/or minced fresh cilantro, to garnish (optional)

DIRECTIONS

1 Melt oil or margarine or butter in a large pot over medium-high heat. Add brown sugar, salt and ginger and stir until combined. Add rice and stir to coat evenly.

2 Pour coconut milk and water into pot with rice and bring to a boil. Place a tight-fitting lid on the pot and reduce the heat to a simmer. Simmer for 20 minutes without disturbing. Do not lift the lid.

3 Remove the pot from the heat and leave the lid in place for an additional 10 minutes. Remove lid and fluff rice with a fork.

4 Top with toasted coconut and scallions and/or cilantro, if using.

pea points

If you omit the scallions and cilantro, this rice can double as a delicious breakfast dish when topped with cinnamon and nondairy milk or organic milk.

NUTRITION INFORMATION PER SERVING: 250 calories, 8 g total fat, 4.5 g saturated fat, 0 g trans fat, 0 mg cholesterol, 180 mg sodium, 40 g carbohydrate, 2 g fiber, 4 g sugar, 4 g protein, vitamin A 0%, vitamin C 0%, calcium 2%, iron 4%

Optional ingredients and toppings not included in analysis.

Snacks, Sides and Sauces

Sweet Potato Dream

Makes 4 servings of approximately 1½ cups each

I GET EMBARRASSED WHEN PEOPLE ASK ME WHAT MY FAVORITE FOOD IS.

I simply can't answer in a way that doesn't make me sound like a complete jerk. The first problem is I am highly indecisive. Then again, maybe I'm not. I can't make up my mind. And I am a foodie, for goodness' sake. I create food on a daily basis. You don't ask Michelangelo what his favorite paint is, do you? See, I told you I'd sound like a complete jerk. Comparing the Sistine Chapel to Mmmm Sauce and Cookie Dough Balls. Some people.

Then you add in the problem of what my actual favorite foods are. It's hard to tell you without making you hate me. It's sort of like when you were in fifth grade and the teacher asked what the capital of Florida was and everyone's guessing Miami and Orlando and you know the right answer is Tallahassee, but again, you don't want to look like a total jerk, so you just keep your mouth shut or, worse still, shout out "St. Petersburg" to fit in.

And I relive it all again when asked about my favorite food. I could go with popular answers and say, "Pizza" or "Chocolate chip cookies." But that would be a straight-up "capital of Florida" lie. Because I'm obsessed with broccoli. I would eat oatmeal for every meal if I could. And most days of the week, I would choose a perfect sweet potato over a piece of wedding cake. What a jerk.

I want you to get it, though, and I think with this recipe, you just might. Sweet potato fries are swell. A baked sweet potato is stellar. And there was once even a time I could get behind the traditional sweet potato casserole, with its syrupy brown sugar and roasted marshmallow topping. But what I've created here with sweet potatoes, well, it's even better. It's a dream come true. And I will proudly say, it's my favorite. When you try it, you can take back that whole jerk thing.

more peas, thank you

INGREDIENTS

2 pounds sweet potatoes, peeled and cut into 2-inch pieces

⅓ cup nondairy milk or organic milk

1 tablespoon vegan margarine (i.e., Earth Balance), coconut oil or organic butter

2 tablespoons light brown sugar

2 tablespoons molasses

½ teaspoon cinnamon

½ teaspoon nutmeg

½ teaspoon salt

Topping:
¼ cup oat flour

¼ cup light brown sugar

2 tablespoons vegan margarine (i.e., Earth Balance) or coconut oil or coconut butter

½ cup pecans or walnuts, chopped

cooking spray, to grease casserole dish

DIRECTIONS

1   Place sweet potatoes in a medium pot and cover with water. Bring to a boil over medium-high heat, cover with a lid and reduce heat. Simmer for 15 to 20 minutes, or until sweet potatoes are soft.

2   Preheat oven to 375 degrees F.

3   Drain sweet potatoes and place in a bowl. Add milk, margarine, coconut oil or butter, brown sugar, molasses, cinnamon, nutmeg and salt. Using an electric handheld mixer or a stand mixer, beat all ingredients together until there are no chunks and potatoes are fluffy.

4   In a small bowl, combine oat flour, brown sugar and margarine, coconut oil or coconut butter to make topping. Mix ingredients together using a fork until mixture has the consistency of coarse crumbs. Stir in nuts.

5   Spread sweet potato mixture in the bottom of a 2-quart casserole dish that has been lightly greased with cooking spray. Sprinkle topping evenly over sweet potatoes.

6   Bake for 40 to 45 minutes, or until topping has browned and potatoes are heated through.

NUTRITION INFORMATION PER SERVING: 500 calories, 18 g total fat, 3.5 g saturated fat, 0 g trans fat, 0 mg cholesterol, 510 mg sodium, 82 g carbohydrate, 9 g fiber, 37 g sugar, 6 g protein, vitamin A 640%, vitamin C 10%, calcium 15%, iron 15%

Carrot Orange Pistachio Streusel Muffins

Makes 12 muffins

NOT EVERY RECIPE IS A SYMPHONY.

I'd love to say that I carefully contemplate what goes into each and everything I cook. Doing nutritional calculations. Balancing flavor profiles. Methodically testing texture, mouth feel and satiety.

You forget a few things. I have laundry. I have a cat that has digestion problems. I have a duvet cover that must be painstakingly removed to be spot cleaned. Usually twice a week. Love that cat. Do I need to remind you that I have kids? And that, strangely enough, they need to be fed? More than twice a week.

When Lulu and I hit the kitchen together for a baking adventure, there's no science involved. The only analysis going on is, "What do we have?" and, almost equally as important, "What do you like?" I open the fridge and simultaneously open a world of possibilities. Pickles can't go in muffins. Neither can cheese, ketchup or green olives. But Lulu likes carrots. She likes oranges. And she loves "mustachios."

Turns out, mustachios are my favorite nut ever. And Lulu's too. So together we came up with a beautiful concoction—a muffin tender and moist from the carrots, with a nice balance of acidity from the orange juice, and of course, studded with those delicious mustachios.

Now that is music to my ears.

79

Snacks, Sides and Sauces

INGREDIENTS

Muffins:

12 paper muffin baking cups

1 cup whole wheat pastry flour

1 cup unbleached all-purpose flour

1 tablespoon baking powder

½ teaspoon baking soda

½ teaspoon salt

½ teaspoon cinnamon

½ teaspoon ground ginger

1 cup carrots, sliced

¼ cup vegan margarine (i.e., Earth Balance) or coconut oil, melted

1 cup orange juice

⅔ cup light brown sugar

1 tablespoon orange zest

½ cup pistachios, chopped

Streusel topping:

2 tablespoons old-fashioned oats

2 tablespoons vegan margarine (i.e., Earth Balance)

2 tablespoons light brown sugar

1 tablespoon organic sugar

½ teaspoon cinnamon

¼ cup pistachios, chopped

DIRECTIONS

1 Preheat oven to 375 degrees F. Line a 12-cup muffin tin with paper baking cups and set aside.

2 In a large bowl, combine flours, baking powder, baking soda, salt, cinnamon and ginger.

3 Steam carrots by covering with water in a microwave-safe bowl and microwaving for 5 to 6 minutes. Alternatively, place carrots in a small saucepan, cover with an inch to 2 inches of water and gently bring to a boil. Cover, lower heat and simmer for 5 to 6 minutes, or until carrots are soft. Add cooked carrots to a high-speed blender or food processor with just enough of the water from the bowl or pot to make a smooth, yet thick puree.

4 To pureed carrots, add margarine or coconut oil, orange juice and brown sugar. Add carrot mixture to dry ingredients, stirring until just combined. Fold in orange zest and pistachios.

5   In a small bowl, blend together oats, margarine, brown sugar, organic sugar and cinnamon with a fork until a crumbly streusel forms. Stir in pistachios.

6   Spoon muffin batter into prepared muffin tin, filling each cup three-quarters of the way full. Sprinkle each muffin with a small spoonful of streusel topping, distributing evenly between muffins.

7   Bake muffins for 18 to 20 minutes, or until a toothpick inserted into the center comes out clean. Store leftover muffins in an airtight container.

NUTRITION INFORMATION PER SERVING: 240 calories, 9 g total fat, 2 g saturated fat, 0 g trans fat, 0 mg cholesterol, 270 mg sodium, 35 g carbohydrate, 3 g fiber, 17 g sugar, 4 g protein, vitamin A 35%, vitamin C 20%, calcium 2%, iron 6%

82

Mmmm Sauces

These sauces are inspired by the delicious Yumm! Sauce made famous by Café Yumm!

THIS RECIPE GOES OUT TO OUR FRIEND SCOTT.

Though he's technically Pea Daddy's friend, Scott and I have a lot in common. We both hate running but do it, anyway. We shouldn't. We both irritate our spouses by reading a blog about Peas via iPhone in our bed each night. We absolutely should. As should you. We both love Yumm! Sauce.

Yumm! Sauce is this fantastic "cheesy," creamy (and *vegan*) sauce that is made, sold and served at a local chain of cafés called Café Yumm! They put it on just about everything they make, from rice bowls to salads to wraps. It's so good, it's drinkable.

I'd tried to make it in the past, but never quite got it right, a fact I mentioned to Scott. He usually skips right over the recipes when reading our site and heads for the jokes (aka fodder with which to razz Pea Daddy) and eagerly said, "Oh my gosh, you make that sauce?"

And so, for Scott, I did. Little did I know that when I made my original Mmmm Sauce and shared it on the blog, not only would Scott go crazy, but my readers would, too. They're making quadruple batches. They're asking for different flavors and varieties. They're drizzling it on salads and stir-fries, slathering it on sandwiches and wraps and, in some cases, drinking it straight from the blender.

As reader Tricia said, "I literally bit the side of my mouth three times the first time I had Mmmm Sauce, because I was eating it as quickly as possible. I was doubled over in pain, only it wasn't as bad while eating Mmmm Sauce, because I had the Mmmm Sauce to soothe me."

Oh, dear.

No matter what you do with Mmmm Sauce, we all have one thing in common—all it takes is one taste and we can't help but say, "Mmmm."

ORIGINAL MMMM SAUCE

Makes approximately 1½ cups of Original Mmmm or 16 responsible
2-tablespoon servings

¼ cup extra-virgin olive oil

¼ cup raw almonds

⅓ cup water

¼ cup cooked chickpeas, drained
and rinsed

¼ cup nutritional yeast

2½ tablespoons lemon juice

1 teaspoon garlic, minced

¼ teaspoon salt

¾ teaspoon curry powder

½ teaspoon dried oregano

½ teaspoon dried cilantro

DIRECTIONS

1   In a high-speed blender or food processor, combine oil, almonds,
    water and chickpeas. Blend until relatively smooth.

2   Add remaining ingredients and blend until smooth.

3   Transfer to a small bowl, cover and refrigerate until serving.

NUTRITION INFORMATION PER SERVING: 60 calories, 4.5 g total fat, 0 g saturated fat,
0 g trans fat, 0 mg cholesterol, 40 mg sodium, 2 g carbohydrate, <1 g fiber, 0 g sugar,
2 g protein, vitamin A 0%, vitamin C 2%, calcium 0%, iron 2%

ORIGINAL MMMM MEAL IDEAS

You can put this sauce on just about anything, but here are some ways you may
not have thought of:

MMMM NACHOS: Build a plate with baked tortilla chips (perhaps make your
own), canned pinto beans, chopped tomatoes, sliced olives, jalapeños and fresh
cilantro, and drizzle Mmmm Sauce over the top.

MAC 'N' MMMM: Cook up some whole wheat or rice macaroni noodles and toss
in Mmmm Sauce. Serve straight from the stove top, or place in a casserole, top
with bread crumbs and bake at 350 degrees F for 15 minutes.

WELSH RAREBIT: Lightly steam some broccoli, cauliflower or asparagus. Toast some thin whole-grain bread. Layer steamed vegetables on top of the toast and drizzle with Mmmm Sauce.

MMMM FONDUE: Heat Mmmm Sauce and keep warm in a fondue pot. Serve with crudités, whole-grain breads, whole wheat pretzels and marinated mushrooms, and dip away!

PEANUT MMMM SAUCE

Makes approximately 1½ cups of Peanut Mmmm or 16 responsible 2-tablespoon servings

½ cup coconut milk (full or reduced fat)

½ cup fire-roasted tomatoes in juice

¼ cup natural peanut butter

3 tablespoons reduced sodium soy sauce

juice of 1 lime

2 teaspoons fresh ginger

1 teaspoon garlic, minced

1 tablespoon agave or maple syrup

sriracha to taste (optional)

DIRECTIONS

1 Combine coconut milk, tomatoes, peanut butter, soy sauce, lime juice, ginger, garlic, sweetener and sriracha, if using, in a food processor or high-speed blender, and blend until smooth.

2 Pour sauce into a small bowl. Cover and refrigerate if not using right away.

NUTRITION INFORMATION PER SERVING: 40 calories, 2.5 g total fat, 0.5 saturated fat, 0 g trans fat, 0 mg cholesterol, 110 mg sodium, 3 g carbohydrate, 0 g fiber, 2 g sugar, 2 g protein, vitamin A 2%, vitamin C 2%, calcium 0%, iron 2%

Optional ingredients and toppings not included in analysis.

Snacks, Sides and Sauces

PEANUT MMMM MEAL IDEAS

Try this sauce over a stir-fry of broccoli, red peppers and carrots tossed with brown rice or rice noodles, or try it in one of these meals:

PEANUT PITA PIZZAS: Spread the sauce over whole wheat pitas. Top with diced red peppers, drained chickpeas and diced pineapple. Bake for 10 to 12 minutes at 425 degrees F.

SALAD ROLLS: Wrap rice noodles, carrots, bean sprouts, mint and tofu in softened rice paper. Use the sauce for dipping.

ASIAN PEANUT SLAW: Add the sauce to 4 to 5 cups of shredded cabbage, shredded carrot, red pepper strips and minced green onion. Toss in tofu or crumbled tempeh for extra oomph.

NACHO MMMM SAUCE

Makes approximately 1½ cups of Nacho Mmmm or 16 responsible 2-tablespoon servings

⅔ cup prepared or homemade salsa

⅓ cup water

¼ cup raw almonds

¼ cup cooked chickpeas, drained and rinsed

¼ cup nutritional yeast

2 tablespoons lemon juice

1 teaspoon garlic, minced

¼ teaspoon salt

1 teaspoon chili powder

1 teaspoon cumin

1 teaspoon dried cilantro or
1 to 2 tablespoons fresh cilantro

DIRECTIONS

1   Combine salsa, water, almonds, chickpeas, nutritional yeast, lemon juice, garlic, salt, chili powder, cumin and cilantro in a food processor or high-speed blender, and blend until smooth.

2   Pour sauce into a medium bowl. Cover and refrigerate until serving.

NUTRITION INFORMATION PER SERVING: 35 calories, 1.5 g total fat, 0 g saturated fat, 0 g trans fat, 0 mg cholesterol, 115 mg sodium, 3 g carbohydrate, <1 g fiber, <1 g sugar, 2 g protein, vitamin A 2%, vitamin C 2%, calcium 2%, iron 2%

NACHO MMMM MEAL IDEAS

Sure, this sauce is perfect for dipping chips in, but it also could be the center of many delicious meals, like:

NACHO MMMM SALAD: Serve the sauce over crisp romaine topped with black beans, tomato, corn, olives, cilantro and avocado. Serve with baked tortilla chips.

NACHO MMMM PIZZA: Top a whole wheat pizza crust with sauce, roasted chickpeas and olives. Bake at 350 degrees F for 15 minutes and then top with tomatoes, lettuce and crushed baked tortilla chips.

NACHO MMMM CHICKPEA SALAD STUFFED PITAS: Mix roasted chickpeas with the sauce. Add chopped peppers and onions, if desired. Stuff inside whole wheat pita pockets and garnish with lettuce.

MAC 'N' CHICKPEAS: Stir the sauce into cooked macaroni, top with crushed, baked tortilla chips and bake at 350 degrees F for 20 to 25 minutes.

PESTO MMMM SAUCE

Makes approximately 1½ cups of Pesto Mmmm or 16 responsible
2-tablespoon servings

1 bunch basil, or approximately
2 cups packed leaves

¼ cup extra-virgin olive oil

⅓ cup walnuts, toasted

⅓ cup water

¼ cup cooked chickpeas, drained
and rinsed

1 tablespoon garlic, minced

1½ tablespoons lemon juice

⅓ cup nutritional yeast

Salt and pepper to taste

DIRECTIONS

1   Combine basil, olive oil, toasted walnuts, water, chickpeas, garlic,
    lemon juice, and nutritional yeast in a food processor or high-speed
    blender, and blend until smooth.

2   Add salt and pepper to taste.

3   Pour sauce into a medium bowl. Cover and refrigerate until serving.

NUTRITION INFORMATION PER SERVING: 50 calories, 4 g total fat, 0.5 g saturated fat,
0 g trans fat, 0 mg cholesterol, 15 mg sodium, 3 g carbohydrate, 1 g fiber, 0 g sugar,
2 g protein, vitamin A 6%, vitamin C 2%, calcium 2%, iron 2%

more peas, thank you

PESTO MMMM MEAL IDEAS

This sauce is fantastic on pasta, but here are some uses that are outside the pasta bowl:

PESTO PIZZA: Smear the sauce on whole wheat pizza dough or pitas and top with roasted veggies, kalamata olives and more toasted walnuts.

PESTO POTATOES: Mix the sauce into mashed potatoes for a green twist on the traditional side dish.

PESTO FRENCH BREAD: Slice open a whole-grain loaf, smear both sides generously with the sauce and bake for 20 minutes at 350 degrees F.

PESTO TOFU: Marinate your tofu in this sauce overnight and then broil it for 6 to 7 minutes on each side for a chewy, herby, protein-packed delight.

Snacks, Sides and Sauces

Salsa Verde

Makes 2½ cups

YOU KNOW WHAT ONE OF THE MOST VERSATILE THINGS IN THE WORLD IS?

A pair of yoga pants. I know, I know. It's so cliché to tell you I live in mine. Especially because I don't do yoga. Ever. I enjoy being able to bend over and pick up a toy the next day if need be. Somebody has to.

On their own, yoga pants can be a little too clingy, a little too stretchy, and at times, if your shirt is short enough, a little obscene. But throw on a long sweater and a pair of ballet flats and you've got yourself a "going to the store" outfit. A "pick Gigi up from school" outfit. A "going to church on Sunday morning" outfit. I'm convinced God doesn't care if I slept in these pants last night. Why should Pea Daddy?

The only thing more versatile than stretchy pants is this salsa. It's a dip for chips. It's a sauce for enchiladas. Throw in some beans, broth and veggies and it's a base for chili.

All in all, it's delicious. And there's nothing obscene about that.

INGREDIENTS

1 pound tomatillos (approximately 5 or 6 large fruits), husked and rinsed

1 lime, juiced

½ cup yellow onion, diced

1 teaspoon garlic, minced

1 jalapeño, seeded and minced (optional)

3 tablespoons fresh cilantro, minced

1 teaspoon dried oregano

1 teaspoon cumin

1 teaspoon salt

DIRECTIONS

1   Place tomatillos, lime juice, onion, garlic, jalapeño (if using), cilantro, oregano, cumin and salt in a blender or food processor and pulse until combined but still chunky. Transfer to a small saucepan and bring to a simmer over medium heat. Continue to simmer for approximately 15 minutes or until tomatillos have given off their juices and the flavors have melded.

pea points

This is the perfect sauce for the Green and Red Lentil Enchiladas in our first book. You may want to make a double batch and freeze half to use when making the easy and delicious Green and White Bean Chili on p. 120.

2 Remove from heat. Cool to room temperature and then chill, covered, before serving.

NUTRITION INFORMATION PER SERVING: 25 calories, 0.5 g total fat, 0 g saturated fat, 0 g trans fat, 0 mg cholesterol, 290 mg sodium, 5 g carbohydrate, 1 g fiber, 3 g sugar, <1 g protein, vitamin A 2%, vitamin C 15%, calcium 2%, iron 4%

Based on 8 servings per recipe. Optional ingredients and toppings not included in analysis.

Better Bay Biscuits

Makes 12 biscuits

These biscuits aren't just like a popular seafood chain's cheddar biscuits. They are better.

I NEVER MET A BREAD BASKET I DIDN'T LIKE.

Especially at chain restaurants. What is it about having unlimited warm, buttery, cheesy baked goods that makes us go crazy? They're free! They're unlimited! They're warm, buttery and cheesy!

So are these biscuits. When I first featured this recipe on our site, it immediately became a reader favorite. As reader Rebekah explained, "I made these for dinner to go with some soup. Holy smokes! They are incredible. So light and fluffy and melt in your mouth. My seven-year-old said, 'I don't think you could possibly make these any better.'"

If I've learned anything in my life, it's not to argue with a seven-year-old and never, ever pass up the bread basket.

more peas, thank you

INGREDIENTS

1 cup whole wheat pastry flour

1 cup unbleached
all-purpose flour

½ teaspoon salt

1 tablespoon organic sugar

1 tablespoon baking powder

½ cup vegan margarine (i.e.,
Earth Balance) or organic butter,
plus 2 tablespoons melted, to
brush on finished biscuits

¾ cup nondairy milk
(unflavored and unsweetened)
or organic milk

¼ teaspoon garlic powder

1 cup shredded nondairy cheddar
cheese (i.e., Daiya)
or organic cheddar cheese

½ teaspoon garlic salt

½ teaspoon dried parsley

DIRECTIONS

1   Preheat oven to 400 degrees F.

2   In a large bowl, combine flours, salt, sugar and baking powder.
    Cut in margarine or butter using a pastry blender, fork or food
    processor. Don't overwork the mixture, but try to get the margarine
    or butter as uniformly incorporated as possible.

3   Stir in milk, garlic powder and cheese and mix until just combined.
    Do not overmix.

4   Using an ice cream scoop or a ¼-cup measuring cup, scoop dough,
    place on an ungreased cookie sheet and press into biscuit shapes.

5   Bake 15 to 17 minutes, or until biscuits have set.

6   In a small bowl, combine melted margarine or butter, garlic salt
    and dried parsley.

7   Allow biscuits to cool slightly and then brush with garlic butter
    or margarine and serve.

NUTRITION INFORMATION PER SERVING: 190 calories, 11 g total fat, 4 g saturated fat,
0 g trans fat, 10 mg cholesterol, 300 mg sodium, 17 g carbohydrate, 2 g fiber, 2 g sugar,
5 g protein, vitamin A 2%, vitamin C 0%, calcium 35%, iron 2%

Quinoa Tabouleh

Makes 4 servings

IT'S MY LIFE'S MISSION TO BRING QUINOA TO THE MASSES.

It's also my life's mission to eat at least one meal a day that features warm, fluffy pita bread, creamy hummus and salty olives.

Tabouleh is a traditional Greek salad, filled with mint, parsley, tomatoes, cucumbers and usually bulgur. Bulgur. Sounds like *vulgar*. But it happens to be a grain that is the same size as quinoa and shares its heartiness.

And thus, this dish is a bridge to both of those life's missions. Let's all cross that bridge together.

INGREDIENTS

2 cups vegetable stock

1 cup quinoa, rinsed and drained

¼ cup extra-virgin olive oil

¼ cup lemon juice

1½ teaspoons salt

½ teaspoon cumin

1½ cups cherry tomatoes, halved

2 small or Persian cucumbers, seeded and chopped

1 cup fresh parsley, minced

¼ cup fresh mint, minced

salt and pepper to taste

DIRECTIONS

1 Bring stock to a boil in a medium saucepan over high heat. Add quinoa, reduce heat to low, cover and simmer for 15 minutes. Remove from heat, let set for several minutes and then fluff with a fork.

2 In a large bowl, combine olive oil, lemon juice, salt and cumin. Add quinoa. Fold in tomatoes, cucumber, parsley and mint. Season with salt and pepper to taste. Chill, covered, until serving.

NUTRITION INFORMATION PER SERVING: 290 calories, 16 g total fat, 2 g saturated fat, 0 g trans fat, 0 mg cholesterol, 1170 mg sodium, 33 g carbohydrate, 4 g fiber, 5 g sugar, 6 g protein, vitamin A 25%, vitamin C 30%, calcium 6%, iron 25%

pea points

For extra protein, toss in some cooked garbanzo beans or leftover tofu. Don't forget the warm pita bread, creamy hummus and salty olives on the side.

Almost Chipotle Guacamole

Makes 4 servings of approximately ¼ cup each

The only thing that makes Chipotle's guacamole better is that you don't have to make it. But now you can.

I HESITATED TO PUT THIS RECIPE IN THE SNACKS, SIDES AND SAUCES CHAPTER OF THIS BOOK, BECAUSE WHENEVER I HAVE THIS GUACA-MOLE, IT TURNS INTO AN ENTRÉE.

Our nearest Chipotle Mexican Grill knows exactly what I'm going to ask for when I show up: extra guacamole. And since I'm skipping the meat, I think they think they owe it to me to give me about four avocados' worth, leaving me with a salad or burrito that is almost entirely rich, creamy green heaven. In other words, awesome.

I knew I had to replicate this deliciousness at home. So Almost Chipotle Guacamole was born. And it hasn't disappointed. Reader Stephanie says, "Before I made this, I didn't think I was a fan of guacamole. Now I can't get enough of it. It is amazing!"

Heap it on, Stephanie. You have my full support.

INGREDIENTS

2 ripe Haas avocados	1½ tablespoons lemon or lime juice	sriracha to taste (optional)
2 tablespoons red onion, finely chopped	½ teaspoon salt	
	2 tablespoons fresh cilantro, chopped	

DIRECTIONS

Mash avocados in a large bowl. Add chopped onion, lemon or lime juice, salt, cilantro and sriracha, if using, and mix well. Adjust seasoning accordingly.

NUTRITION INFORMATION PER SERVING: 190 calories, 15 g total fat, 3 g saturated fat, 0 g trans fat, 0 mg cholesterol, 300 mg sodium, 13 g carbohydrate, 9 g fiber, 4 g sugar, 3 g protein, vitamin A 4%, vitamin C 45%, calcium 2%, iron 2%

Optional ingredients and toppings not included in analysis.

Cracklin' Cauliflower

Serves 4 or 1—your call
This dish is quite similar to Whole Foods' version, although unfortunately, you can't buy it by the pound. Good for your pocketbook, bad for your new addiction.

NOT EVERYONE IS A FAN OF CAULIFLOWER AND I TOTALLY GET THAT.

It's one strange vegetable, with all the joys that come with crucifers and the added bonus that when cooked up, it sort of looks like little brains. I'm not doing much to sell you on making this recipe, am I?

I turned the corner with cauliflower myself at a Whole Foods hot bar. This amazing curry-sauced dish, topped rather appropriately with peas, caught my eye, and it was love at first bite. My devotion only grew when I replicated the dish at home. The only problem was, the rest of the Peas wanted in on the action, and frankly, I have no problem putting away the whole recipe by myself. Sharing hurts. Reader Diedhre agrees, saying, "I never thought I liked cauliflower. I have been converted. My husband even ate seconds! It's positively addicting!"

Maybe you should stay quiet about this recipe when you make it, thereby allowing bigger servings for yourself. Or just tell your family cauliflower is icky and looks like brains.

INGREDIENTS

1 medium head cauliflower, trimmed and cut into florets

1 to 2 teaspoons olive oil

½ teaspoon salt

1½ teaspoons curry powder

½ teaspoon garam masala

3 tablespoons yellow onion, chopped

2 cloves garlic, minced

2 teaspoons fresh ginger, minced

½ cup frozen peas

1 teaspoon lemon zest

pinch of sugar or stevia

salt and pepper to taste

fresh cilantro, to garnish (optional)

DIRECTIONS

1 Preheat oven to 400 degrees F.

2 Put cauliflower florets in a large bowl and drizzle with olive oil, tossing to coat.

3 Add salt, curry and garam masala, and stir to coat. Add onion, garlic, ginger, peas and lemon zest and mix thoroughly.

4 Season to taste with sugar or stevia, salt and pepper and mix well. Transfer to a medium baking dish and bake for 30 minutes, stirring every 10 minutes to ensure even roasting.

5 Garnish with fresh cilantro and serve.

NUTRITION INFORMATION PER SERVING: 70 calories, 2.5 g total fat, 0 g saturated fat, 0 g trans fat, 0 mg cholesterol, 60 mg sodium, 10 g carbohydrate, 4 g fiber, 4 g sugar, 4 g protein, vitamin A 10%, vitamin C 130%, calcium 4%, iron 6%

Optional ingredients and toppings not included in analysis.

Soups, Salads and Sandwiches

Superb Spinach Salad 102

Carib"bean"
Pumpkin Soup 105

Jicama Grapefruit
Salad 108

Corn Chowda with
Corn Bread Croutons 110

Ginger Soy Soup 112

Moroccan
Chickpea Stew 115

Tofu Noodle Soup 118

Green and White
Bean Chili 120

Red Lentil Soup 122

Cucumber Quinoa
Salad 125

Cowboy Caviar 127

Tortilla Soup 130

Chickpea Melts 132

Sunshine Kale Salad 134

Superb Spinach Salad

Makes 4 entrée-size salads
This salad was inspired by Trader Joe's Super Spinach Salad.

I ALWAYS WANTED TO HAVE GIRLS.

As a girl myself, I thought I'd know exactly what to do with a girl, at least in the biological sense. I'm relieved I've never had to make crucial decisions regarding certain male body parts. I'm still not entirely certain what goes on down there between the time your son is born and when you take him home from the hospital, and it's a category of knowledge I'm happy to be ignorant about. Unless, of course, I'm ever on *Jeopardy!* and "Circumcision" is a category. Both of those are exceedingly unlikely.

I also appreciate that I've never had to potty train a boy. I've heard horror stories of little guys marking their territory, watering indoor plants and toy boxes. My girls stuck to their potties. And by "potties," I mean our carpet. Feel free to keep your shoes on next time you come over.

I thought I knew what to do with girls. But I underestimated what a tomboy I truly was. My girls want to have tea parties. Play dress up. Paint toenails. Braid hair. Buy pink shoes, pink tights, pink skirts, pink dresses and pink shirts, and don't forget to top it all off with pink bows. I've created monsters. Beautiful pink monsters, naturally.

I appreciate that they take pride in their appearance. I love that they are confident. But somehow, somewhere, we've crossed a line. I realize it every time I have to pull them away from their reflection in the fireplace glass, the oven window or the rearview mirror. No, really—pull them away. Somehow I don't think boys do that.

On a recent afternoon I started making a spinach quinoa salad, much like a version I picked up in the ready-made case of our favorite grocery store. I grabbed the Super Spinach Salad in a fit of hunger, dashing between preschool and ballet practice. Thankfully, Lulu saved me the trouble of needing to change her into her tutu by insisting on wearing it to school, with flannel pajama pants and rain boots, of course. And though the store-made salad's spinach was a bit wilted and the dressing had separated into an oil slick, it was still delicious. And I'm sure that had nothing to do with the early morning carpooling that had me willing to eat a shoe. A pink shoe.

Still, I was inspired to make this salad at home and make it, well, prettier. As I layered the ingredients in the bowl—bright, crisp greens and striking cherry tomatoes—I couldn't help but admire my creation.

"Beautiful!" I cried out.

"Me?" asked Gigi.

Sure, kid.

I whipped up a batch of creamy orange dressing to drizzle over the top and praised the dish again.

"Beautiful!" I exclaimed.

"Me?" asked Lulu.

Sure, you too.

I always wanted to have girls. And I wouldn't trade those beautiful girls of mine for anything. Except maybe a superb spinach salad. Hold the pink.

INGREDIENTS

½ cup dry quinoa, rinsed and drained

1 cup low-sodium vegetable stock

salt to taste

6 cups organic baby spinach

1 cup edamame, shelled

1 cup cooked chickpeas, drained and rinsed

1 cup organic cherry tomatoes, halved

½ cup dried cranberries

½ cup pumpkin seeds, raw or roasted

Carrot Miso Dressing:
1½ cups carrots, chopped

2 tablespoons fresh ginger, minced

2 tablespoons rice vinegar

2 tablespoons white or yellow miso

2 tablespoons sesame oil

1 tablespoon canola oil

1 teaspoon mirin

¼ cup water

DIRECTIONS

1   Place quinoa and broth in a small saucepan and bring to a boil. Reduce heat, cover and simmer for 15 to 20 minutes, or until liquid is absorbed and quinoa can be fluffed with a fork. Season with salt to taste. Set aside to cool.

2   To prepare the dressing, combine carrots, ginger, vinegar, miso, sesame oil, canola oil, mirin and water in a food processor or blender and blend until smooth. Refrigerate until serving.

3   To build the salad, place spinach in the bottom of a large serving bowl. Top with cooled quinoa, edamame, chickpeas, cherry tomatoes, dried cranberries and pumpkin seeds. Serve with Carrot Miso Dressing.

NUTRITION INFORMATION PER SERVING: 430 calories, 23 g total fat, 3.5 g saturated fat, 0 g trans fat, 0 mg cholesterol, 740 mg sodium, 45 g carbohydrate, 9 g fiber, 7 g sugar, 16 g protein, vitamin A 250%, vitamin C 45%, calcium 15%, iron 40%

Analysis includes Carrot Miso Dressing.

Carib"bean" Pumpkin Soup

Makes 6 servings of approximately 1½ cups each

HEY, MON.

There is nothing I like better in the dead of winter than a nice piping bowl of soup. That's not entirely true. I like a nice vacation to somewhere warmer, somewhere drier and somewhere where there are no New Year's resolutions to stop watching unscripted TV and to start reading more books that have more words than pictures. This book may just barely make that cut. Phew.

This soup is the best of both worlds. Hearty and satisfying to stave off the cold, but if you listen carefully after spooning it up, you can faintly hear the palm trees rustling in the breeze. Or maybe you're just watching *Survivor* like me.

Either way, here's your postcard in a bowl, Mon.

INGREDIENTS

1 teaspoon coconut oil or cooking spray

1 medium yellow onion, chopped

1 cup carrots, chopped

1 cup celery, chopped

¼ medium banana, chopped

1 clove garlic, minced

1 tablespoon fresh ginger, minced

1 teaspoon nutmeg

1½ teaspoons cinnamon

¼ teaspoon allspice

1 teaspoon curry powder

3 cups vegetable broth

1 14-ounce can of reduced-fat coconut milk

1½ cups canned pumpkin

1 14-ounce can white or pinto beans, drained and rinsed

agave nectar or stevia to taste (optional)

salt and pepper to taste

nondairy sour cream or organic dairy sour cream, to garnish (optional)

toasted coconut, to garnish (optional)

DIRECTIONS

1 Place a large stockpot over medium-high heat and melt coconut oil. Or grease stockpot with cooking spray before placing it on the heat. Add onion, carrot and celery. Sauté for 5 to 6 minutes, or until onion is translucent and starts to brown and veggies are tender.

2 Add banana, garlic, ginger, nutmeg, cinnamon, allspice and curry powder and sauté for an additional 1 to 2 minutes, or until aromatic.

3 Add vegetable broth, coconut milk, pumpkin and beans and bring to a low boil. Reduce heat to low and simmer for 15 to 20 minutes.

4 Allow soup to cool slightly and then transfer half to a high-speed blender, pureeing until smooth. Return smooth soup to the pot and repeat process, if necessary, to reach desired consistency. Alternatively, use an immersion blender directly in the pot to reach desired consistency.

5 Add sweetener, if using, and salt and pepper to taste. Pass around sour cream and toasted coconut at the table to garnish the soup.

NUTRITION INFORMATION PER SERVING: 130 calories, 2 g total fat, 1 g saturated fat, 0 g trans fat, 0 mg cholesterol, 670 mg sodium, 25 g carbohydrate, 7 g fiber, 7 g sugar, 5 g protein, vitamin A 260%, vitamin C 10%, calcium 8%, iron 15%

Optional ingredients and toppings not included in analysis.

pea points

Though it may seem out of place, don't leave out the banana. It gives the soup a subtle sweetness and a tropical flavor you'll love.

Soups, Salads and Sandwiches

Jicama Grapefruit Salad

Makes 4 servings
This salad was inspired by the Ensalata De Jicama Y Aguacate Salad at Mijita Cocina Mexicana in San Francisco, California.

YOU KNOW THE BEST TYPE OF RESTAURANT MEALS?

The kind that aren't off the kids' menu. In fact, there isn't even a kids' menu available for the offering, because if it is a memorable restaurant meal, there are no kids around.

No offense, kids, but I have a hard time remembering any meal eaten outside of my home, in a public place, with my girls in tow. You see, the focus isn't on me eating. It's on how much ketchup is being dumped on the table, how many crackers have been crushed into the carpet and how many peas are wedged in between the seat and the back cushion of our booth. It's on how many packets of sugar Gigi is adding to her glass of water. It's on how loudly Lulu is demanding extra pickles on the side.

This recipe is based on a beautiful salad I had on a recent trip to San Francisco. I have effectively replicated it only because it was a trip I took alone.

And it was delicious.

INGREDIENTS

Dressing:
¼ cup reduced-sodium soy sauce

2 tablespoons water

2 limes, juiced

1 teaspoon cumin

1 teaspoon chili powder

agave or stevia to taste

1 cup fresh cilantro, minced

1 large or 2 medium jicama, peeled and cut into ½-inch sticks

2 ruby red grapefruits, peeled and cut into sections

2 avocados, peeled, pitted and sliced

½ cup pumpkin seeds, toasted

DIRECTIONS

1 Whisk together soy sauce, water, lime juice, cumin, chili powder, sweetener and cilantro in a large salad bowl.

2 Add jicama and grapefruit and toss to coat evenly.

3 Plate salad and top with sliced avocado and pumpkin seeds.

NUTRITION INFORMATION PER SERVING: 370 calories, 22 g total fat, 3.5 g saturated fat, 0 g trans fat, 0 mg cholesterol, 590 mg sodium, 41 g carbohydrate, 18 g fiber, 6 g sugar, 10 g protein, vitamin A 20%, vitamin C 170%, calcium 8%, iron 30%

Corn Chowda with Corn Bread Croutons

Makes 6 servings of approximately 1½ cups each

SOMETIMES YOU JUST WANT A THICK, CREAMY CHOWDER.

So legitimate you drop the *er* and add an *a*. Something that will stick to your ribs and that won't turn your crackers into mush. Something that you could eat with a spoon or a fork or, if you're feeling really crazy, a spork. This chowda doesn't call for saltines or for sipping. This chowda calls for croutons and for a big, sturdy bowl, almost too heavy to lift. Leave your dainty soup spoon and your *er* at home. Tonight we eat chowda!

INGREDIENTS

1 cup raw cashews, soaked in water for an hour, then drained

2 teaspoons vegan margarine (i.e., Earth Balance), olive oil or organic butter

1 cup yellow onion, diced

1 teaspoon garlic, minced

¾ teaspoon dried thyme

3 tablespoons finely ground oat flour

4 cups vegetable stock

1 large potato, peeled and diced

4 cups fresh or frozen corn kernels (roasted, if available)

salt and pepper to taste

Corn Bread Croutons (see note on p. 111) and minced fresh parsley, to garnish

DIRECTIONS

1 Heat margarine or oil or butter in a large stockpot over medium-high heat. Add onion and sauté until softened, about 7 minutes.

2 Add garlic and thyme and sauté for an additional minute. Sprinkle vegetables with oat flour and stir to coat. Add vegetable stock and bring to a boil. Add potatoes and boil for about 7 minutes, until potatoes have softened.

more peas, thank you

3   Remove soup from the heat and add cashews. Blend soup in an upright blender or with an immersion blender until smooth and thick.

4   Return soup to the pot and add corn. Season with salt and pepper and simmer over low heat until kernels are tender, about 10 minutes for fresh corn and about 5 minutes for frozen.

5   Spoon soup into bowls and top with Corn Bread Croutons and fresh parsley.

Note: For Corn Bread Croutons, preheat oven to 400 degrees F. Cut corn bread, either store-bought or prepared using your favorite recipe (ahem, Cowgirl Cornbread from *Peas and Thank You*), into 1- to 2-inch cubes. Spread cubes on a baking sheet that has been lined with parchment or sprayed with cooking spray, and season with salt and pepper, if desired. Bake for 10 to 12 minutes, or until crispy, turning croutons once during cooking.

NUTRITION INFORMATION PER SERVING: 350 calories, 14 g total fat, 3 g saturated fat, 0 g trans fat, <5 mg cholesterol, 470 mg sodium, 54 g carbohydrate, 5 g fiber, 5 g sugar, 10 g protein, vitamin A 0%, vitamin C 25%, calcium 4%, iron 15%

Ginger Soy Soup

Makes 4 large servings of approximately 2 cups each
Just like the soup from the world's best salad bar buffet. Now all we need is the Cookie Lady.

WE DON'T EAT OUT MUCH IN OUR HOUSE.

Think about it. You wouldn't either. Aside from the fact that I make a living each day by cooking, it pains me to pay restaurant prices for food that I can make even more deliciously at home. (Actual age: thirty-four. Age indicated by that sentence: eighty-four.)

There is one restaurant, though, that I don't mind paying for. And there are exactly two reasons why:

1 Weekly coupons; and

2 All-you-can-eat vegetables.

Is that a challenge? They try to inconvenience me by placing the salad bar at the entrance, assuming that most patrons will make one trip through the roughage and then stick to the pizza and pasta, as Pea Daddy and the girls do. I laugh at your silly obstacle! I make at least one return trip to the salad bar each time we are there. In fact, the only time I break from loading two plates at once is when the soup is in my sight.

The dedication to getting our money's worth must run in the family. Not only does our favorite restaurant offer unlimited salads, soups, pastas, pizza, fruit and pack mules, but there, too, is a "Cookie Lady," who makes the rounds, handing out "free" chocolate chip cookies to each table. Whenever my parents come to dinner with us (i.e., when we have extra coupons), my mom stalks the "Cookie Lady" or anyone who may have come within a one-hundred-foot radius of the "Cookie Lady" in the last hour.

"Excuse me, but has the Cookie Lady been around yet?"

"Wait, are you the Cookie Lady?"

"I have a very rare terminal disease, and the only hope I have for survival is cookies, but not any cookie. Only free, mediocre cookies from the Cookie Lady. Save me."

I'm usually hiding in line at the salad bar as this all goes down. Maybe out of embarrassment, Gigi has started making the return trip with me. I couldn't be prouder. And she's started to get as excited as I do when my very favorite soup is in the rotation: their Asian Ginger Broth.

And now I can make it even more delicious at home. Just don't ask me to walk around with a basket of cookies. But you are always welcome to seconds.

INGREDIENTS

1 teaspoon sesame oil

2 tablespoons fresh ginger, minced

1½ tablespoons garlic, minced

8 cups vegetable broth, divided

3 tablespoons cornstarch

2 tablespoons soy sauce or tamari, or more to taste

8 wonton wrappers

cooking spray or oil, to grease baking sheet

sea salt for sprinkling

1 large carrot, cut into matchsticks

1 cup mushrooms, chopped

2 green onions, thinly sliced

1 cup spinach, chopped

1 cup cubed extra-firm tofu

DIRECTIONS

1   To prepare the broth, heat oil in a large stockpot over medium-high heat. Add ginger and garlic and sauté for 1 minute. Add 7 cups of the broth and bring to a low boil.

2   Mix remaining cup of broth with cornstarch in a small bowl and whisk until smooth.

3   Add cornstarch mixture to stockpot and boil, stirring constantly until it thickens. Lower heat and simmer for 10 to 15 minutes.

4   Add soy sauce or tamari and adjust to taste.

5   Meanwhile, preheat the oven to 400 degrees F.

6   Cut each wonton wrapper into 4 strips and place on a baking sheet that has been lightly oiled or sprayed with cooking spray. Sprinkle wonton strips with sea salt.

7   Bake for 4 to 5 minutes, turning halfway through, or until wonton strips have browned and crisped.

8   Place carrots, mushrooms, green onions, spinach, tofu and wonton strips in small serving bowls and arrange on the table. Ladle broth into soup bowls and let everyone build their own bowl with the toppings of their choice.

NUTRITION INFORMATION PER SERVING: 220 calories, 4.5 g total fat, 1 g saturated fat, 0 g trans fat, 0 mg cholesterol, 1650 mg sodium, 37 g carbohydrate, 2 g fiber, 12 g sugar, 9 g protein, vitamin A 120%, vitamin C 15%, calcium 15%, iron 10%

Moroccan Chickpea Stew

Makes 4 servings of approximately 2 cups each

MY MOM IS A STUBBORN WOMAN, BLESS HER HEART.

Someone once told me that you can get away with saying anything about anyone if you always bless their heart afterward. I hope my mom sees it that way, bless her heart.

There are, no doubt, deep psychological reasons for my mom's resistance to change, but those are her stories to tell, not mine. But she'd have to get an actual word processing program on her very large computer. And then, inevitably, she'd call—on her landline, of course—and complain that she couldn't work on her book, because my blog had stalled her computer with all the pictures that took three hours to download on her dial-up internet. She keeps the dial-up so she can use her provider, which blocks all sorts of racy material. Like any video I post on my blog. Bless her heart.

So you can imagine that when I sprung it on my mom that we weren't going to be eating meat anymore, she was more than a little unnerved. How could we have Easter without a ham? How could we eat Sunday dinner's green beans without bacon? How could we go hunting for a Christmas tree and not come back and have cream of potato soup with ham and bacon?

The next year we went tree hunting, we came home and ate this stew. My poor mom. I forgot she doesn't like chickpeas. Or zucchini. Or cooked tomatoes. But she tries. She bought several dozen copies of our first book and gives them proudly to neighbors and friends and little old ladies at the grocery store. And she tells them they can add chicken to all my recipes. Bless her heart.

I'm sure someday when she writes her memoir, she'll tell a tale of being tortured by her hippie daughter with her fancy computer, her newfangled phone and her risqué videos. But most of all by her exotic stews, which, though warming to the soul, spit in the face of tradition. Her tradition. Which just so happens to be filled with cream and ham and bacon.

Bless her heart.

INGREDIENTS

cooking spray or oil, to grease skillet

1 large yellow onion, chopped

2 medium carrots, peeled and chopped

2 teaspoons cumin

1 teaspoon ground, dried ginger

1 teaspoon garlic, minced

1 14-ounce can chickpeas, drained and rinsed

1 14-ounce can fire-roasted tomatoes, drained

1 cup vegetable broth

1 medium zucchini, diced

½ cup raisins or chopped dried apricots

minced fresh parsley, chopped almonds, nondairy or organic dairy Greek yogurt, to garnish (optional)

DIRECTIONS

1 Place a large skillet that has been greased with cooking spray or oil over medium-high heat. Add onion and carrots and sauté until they have softened and started to brown, about 5 to 6 minutes. Add cumin, ginger and garlic to the skillet and sauté for an additional minute. Add chickpeas, tomatoes, vegetable broth, zucchini and raisins or apricots, and cook until heated through and flavors have melded, about 15 to 20 minutes.

2 Place parsley, chopped nuts and yogurt in small serving bowls and arrange on the table. Ladle stew into soup bowls and let everyone add the toppings of their choice. Serve over quinoa or rice, if desired.

NUTRITION INFORMATION PER SERVING: 210 calories, 2 g total fat, 0 g saturated fat, 0 g trans fat, 0 mg cholesterol, 880 mg sodium, 43 g carbohydrate, 9 g fiber, 10 g sugar, 8 g protein, vitamin A 170%, vitamin C 40%, calcium 8%, iron 25%

Optional ingredients and toppings not included in analysis.

Soups, Salads and Sandwiches

Tofu Noodle Soup

Makes 6 servings of approximately 1½ cups each

I WAS PRETTY LUCKY TO GROW UP EATING A LOT OF REALLY GREAT HOME COOKING.

I didn't figure this out until I had to fend for myself later in life. Turns out a package of Red Vines and a sugar-free yogurt not only completely defy logic, but are also a really, really bad lunch choice.

My brother, on the other hand, clued into the beauty of brown bag sandwiches made on homemade honey wheat bread earlier, and used this realization to do what he does best. Shuck and jive. Fast Eddie was turning a pretty profit in the cafeteria, opening his letterman's jacket to expose what Mom had packed for the day and taking cash from the highest bidder.

The biggest wake-up call for me in home cooking appreciation, beyond refined sugar–fueled energy crashes, was how completely lousy canned soup really is. I get sad when I hear people say, "I had a can of soup for dinner." You poor, poor thing. Those sodium-packed, watery, mushy-vegetable, tinny-tasting soups are punishment. You deserve better.

But when you are sick, you want soup. So what are you going to do? Don't you dare open that can. I'll tell you what you're going to do. You're going to do what your mom would do. You're going to get out a big pot. You're going to cook up some fresh chopped vegetables. You're going to fill the pot with a warm, soothing broth. You're going to add a pinch of basil here and a dash of oregano there. You're going to float in giant piles of tender, delicious noodles. And, just to pull a switcheroo on old mom, you're going to toss in some chopped tofu.

Grab your box of tissues, the quilt your grandma made you, a pair of cozy slipper socks and a big bowl of soup. Settle in on your couch and eat your way better. Or watch a Julia Roberts movie your way better. The two are not mutually exclusive.

And then do what any smart person would do. Take your leftovers to work tomorrow and sell them. Cash only.

more peas, thank you

INGREDIENTS

1½ cups dried pasta (use traditional noodles or look for whole-grain varieties in fun shapes, such as corkscrews, fusilli, bow ties)

1 tablespoon vegan margarine (i.e., Earth Balance)

½ cup yellow onion, chopped

½ cup celery, chopped

1 cup carrots, sliced

6 cups vegetable broth

8 ounces baked tofu, cubed

½ teaspoon dried basil

½ teaspoon dried oregano

salt and pepper to taste

DIRECTIONS

1 Bring a large pot of water to boil and cook pasta according to package directions. Drain and set aside.

2 Place a large stockpot over medium-high heat and add vegan margarine. When margarine has melted, add onion, celery and carrots and sauté until tender, about 5 to 6 minutes.

3 Add vegetable broth and bring to a low boil. Reduce heat and add tofu, basil and oregano. Simmer until tofu has heated through. Add noodles, season soup with salt and pepper to taste, and serve.

NUTRITION INFORMATION PER SERVING: 140 calories, 6 g total fat, 1 g saturated fat, 0 g trans fat, 0 mg cholesterol, 640 mg sodium, 17 g carbohydrate, 3 g fiber, 6 g sugar, 8 g protein, vitamin A 70%, vitamin C 4%, calcium 30%, iron 8%

pea points

I always cook my noodles separately from my soup. This keeps the broth from getting too starchy, and then each person can also control how many noodles he or she wants. Lulu lives for noodles. And cheese and pickles.

Soups, Salads and Sandwiches

Green and White Bean Chili

Makes 6 servings of approximately 1½ cups each

I LOVE A GOOD SHORTCUT.

I've got things to do and you do, too. Laundry doesn't just fold itself, lunches don't pack themselves, and even though it's perfectly reasonable to believe that a bedtime story can be read by someone or *something* other than me, I don't like it when my iPhone gets all sticky. Plus, why should technology have all the fun?

I don't want to miss the good stuff because I'm making dinner. I want to stop by the park on the way home. I want to help find the last piece of the jigsaw puzzle, even though I don't like puzzles. I want to give a hand with the math homework, even though I can't remember the last time I didn't have a calculator (with a sticky screen) available.

And since this chili is halfway made before you even start, you'll have plenty of time to do all those things that matter and more. Like cleaning touch screens.

INGREDIENTS

cooking spray or oil, to grease pot

1 medium yellow onion, chopped

1 teaspoon garlic, minced

2 cups vegetable broth

1 tablespoon cornstarch

1½ cups Salsa Verde (p. 90)

1 14-ounce can diced fire-roasted tomatoes

½ teaspoon dried oregano

½ teaspoon cumin

2 15-ounce cans white beans, drained and rinsed

salt and pepper to taste

organic or nondairy sour cream, minced fresh cilantro, lime wedges, to garnish (optional)

DIRECTIONS

1   Grease a large pot with cooking spray or oil and place over medium-high heat. Add onions and sauté until they have softened and started to brown, about 4 to 5 minutes. Add garlic and sauté for an additional minute. Remove pot from heat.

2   In a small bowl, whisk together vegetable broth and cornstarch until there are no lumps.

3   Add broth mixture to the pot and return to heat. Add Salsa Verde, tomatoes, oregano, cumin and beans and bring to a low boil. Simmer for 15 to 20 minutes, or until thickened and heated through.

4   Add salt and pepper to taste and serve with desired toppings.

NUTRITION INFORMATION PER SERVING: 150 calories, 0.5 g total fat, 0 g saturated fat, 0 g trans fat, 0 mg cholesterol, 1080 mg sodium, 36 g carbohydrate, 8 g fiber, 8 g sugar, 9 g protein, vitamin A 10%, vitamin C 25%, calcium 8%, iron 10%

Optional ingredients and toppings not included in analysis.

Soups, Salads and Sandwiches

Red Lentil Soup

Makes 6 servings of approximately 2 cups each

STUDIES SHOW THAT PRESCHOOL-AGED CHILDREN GET AN AVERAGE OF NINE COLDS A YEAR.

The nonscientific explanation has to do with my girls picking their... friends. And their friends get sick a lot. Doing the rather complicated math, that means I am exposed to an average of eighteen colds a year. Good gravy. One and a half colds per month! Put the soup on.

Just when I thought I had enough reasons to come up with another soup recipe (cough, cough), Gigi gave me four more. In the form of her front teeth. Top and bottom. The coming-of-age would be the reasonable explanation. Gigi, on the way to the ER, had another explanation.

"Mom, I wath juth pretending!"

"With a towel on your head, walking into the fence! Pretending what, Geeg?"

"I wath pretending to be a beath towel!"

Well, of course you were.

And so, we eat a lot of soup. It has to be quick. It has to be easy. It has to be delicious. And if you can slip in a little fruit (via oranges) and something pink (via red lentils)? That's right up Gigi's alley.

Her very wide, very toothless alley. Best-looking beach towel in town.

INGREDIENTS

cooking spray or oil, to grease stockpot

1 cup yellow onion, chopped

1 cup celery, chopped

2 medium carrots, peeled and chopped

1 tablespoon cumin

½ teaspoon turmeric

1 teaspoon smoked paprika

2 teaspoons garlic, minced

4 cups vegetable stock

⅓ cup orange juice

1 cup red lentils, picked over and rinsed

1 teaspoon salt

1 tablespoon orange zest

½ cup fresh cilantro, minced

½ cup nondairy or organic dairy sour cream (optional)

DIRECTIONS

1 Lightly coat a large stockpot with cooking spray or oil and place over medium-high heat. Add onion, celery and carrots and sauté until softened, about 5 to 6 minutes.

2 Add cumin, turmeric, smoked paprika and garlic and cook until aromatic, about 1 minute. Pour in vegetable stock and orange juice. Add lentils and salt and bring to a boil.

3 Cover pot and reduce heat to a simmer. Cook for 13 to 15 minutes, or until lentils are soft. Stir in orange zest. Carefully transfer soup to a large blender or use an immersion blender to puree until completely smooth.

4 Serve soup with cilantro and nondairy or organic dairy sour cream as garnishes, if desired.

NUTRITION INFORMATION PER SERVING: 170 calories, 1 g total fat, 0 g saturated fat, 0 g trans fat, 0 mg cholesterol, 810 mg sodium, 31 g carbohydrate, 11 g fiber, 3 g sugar, 10 g protein, vitamin A 80%, vitamin C 20%, calcium 6%, iron 20%

Optional ingredients and toppings not included in analysis.

pea points

If you have fresh lemons on hand, they sub nicely for the orange juice and orange zest in this soup.

Cucumber Quinoa Salad

Makes 4 servings

IF YOU'VE EVER LOST SOMEONE YOU WERE REALLY CLOSE TO, CHANCES ARE YOU HAVE CONVERSATIONS WITH THEM STILL.

Please tell me you do, because it will make me seem a little bit less crazy. My grandma's been gone eight years now, but I still hear her voice as plain as day. And I know exactly what she'd say upon learning that I now write cookbooks and actually cook, multiple times a day, and pretty well, if I do say so myself. She'd say, "Sissy! I never knew you had it in you!"

Because when my grandma was alive, I was no cook. But I didn't have to be. She was alive. This meant that if you had a mouth and could stomach driving to her house and the occasional barb at your expense, you always had something to eat. And plenty to take home. She was honest to a fault, but sweet and generous. She filled the room with her presence, her laughter and her stories, all while she filled your belly with the freshest, most delicious food I've ever eaten.

Their garden overflowed each summer with sweet corn that burst off the cob, string beans, tomatoes, more apples than you could make a thousand pies out of and cucumbers that couldn't taste better than they did right off of the vine. Yet somehow Grandma did make them taste better.

I watched her long fingers work over cucumber after cucumber with a quick peeler, stacking them naked in a neat pile next to the sink. She'd take a large bowl and fill it with vinegar, water, sugar, salt and pepper and then, with a paring knife, methodically make her way through each cucumber, plunking each slice into the brine. That bowl would sit in the fridge for days upon days, and every time we'd eat down to the bottom, Grandma would get out her peeler and start making more cucumber slices to throw into the bowl.

I'm sure my grandma wouldn't have the slightest idea what quinoa is, let alone how to pronounce it. And though she'd shake her head and click her tongue at me for buying cucumbers at the store instead of taking an old grocery sack full from Papa, I think she'd like this salad.

And she'd say, "Sissy, I didn't know you had it in you."

INGREDIENTS

1 cup quinoa, rinsed and drained

1½ cups vegetable broth

2 medium cucumbers, peeled and diced

1 medium red, orange or yellow bell pepper, seeded and diced

1 shallot, minced

2 tablespoons lime juice

¼ cup grapeseed oil

¼ cup water

1-inch fresh ginger, peeled and minced

stevia, agave or honey to taste

salt and pepper to taste

½ cup sesame seeds

DIRECTIONS

1   Combine the quinoa and vegetable broth in a medium-size pot. Bring to a boil over medium-high heat. Cover, lower heat and simmer for 15 to 17 minutes, or until all the broth is absorbed. Remove from heat and allow pot to sit for 10 minutes, covered. Remove lid and fluff quinoa with a fork.

2   If desired, you can chill the quinoa for an hour or so to prepare a cold salad. Add diced cucumbers and bell pepper to quinoa and stir to combine well.

3   To prepare the dressing, combine shallot, lime juice, oil, water, ginger and sweetener in a food processor or blender and blend well. Add salt and pepper to taste. Pour dressing over quinoa and toss.

4   This salad is even better when allowed to marinate for an hour or more. Top with sesame seeds before serving.

NUTRITION INFORMATION PER SERVING: 410 calories, 27 g total fat, 3 g saturated fat, 0 g trans fat, 0 mg cholesterol, 240 mg sodium, 37 g carbohydrate, 6 g fiber, 3 g sugar, 10 g protein, vitamin A 6%, vitamin C 50%, calcium 6%, iron 25%

Cowboy Caviar

Makes 4 servings of approximately 1 cup each

MY YEAR DID NOT GET OFF TO THE LUCKIEST OF STARTS.

Starting January 1, while packing up all our Christmas decorations, putting our gingerbread house and painted pinecones decorated with Red Hots in the safest of places, Gigi made an upsetting discovery. (Note: the recycling bin is a very, very safe place.) She found not one, but two Christmas Karaoke Microphones, which my dear aunt gave the girls for Christmas. I had, unfortunately, *not* put them in the safest of places. (Pea Daddy's workbench, though rarely used for work of any kind, is *not* a very, very safe place.)

And then my stroke of bad luck continued, because the girls made up for lost time with their Christmas Karaoke Microphones.

In the morning, my every move was given a muffled, feedback-riddled play-by-play. "And Mommy is flipping the French toast. Now she's getting out the maple syrup and I don't want water. I want orange juice!" All said to a really horrid Muzak version of "We Wish You a Merry Christmas."

At dinner, saying grace was amplified. "Thank you for this food and everything you did for us and please keep us healthy and safe. Amen!" With "Silent Night" in the background.

After dinner, bedtime stories were read at 140 decibels. "Once upon a time!" "Jingle bells…jingle bells…jingle all the way…"

I'm not one to believe in superstitions, but if eating black-eyed peas for New Year's is going to change my luck, at this point, I'm willing to try anything. This recipe is a simple and delicious way to do it.

Joy to the world!

INGREDIENTS

2 medium bell peppers, any color, seeded and diced

¼ cup yellow onion, minced

1 cup corn (fresh or frozen)

1 tablespoon fresh parsley, chopped

1 14-ounce can black-eyed peas (or any other canned bean), drained and rinsed

salt and pepper to taste

Dressing:
¼ cup seasoned rice vinegar

3 tablespoons balsamic vinegar

2 tablespoons extra-virgin olive oil

1 tablespoon water

1 teaspoon garlic, minced

½ teaspoon cumin

½ teaspoon chili powder

½ teaspoon salt

DIRECTIONS

1   In a large bowl, combine peppers, onion, corn and parsley. There's no need to defrost the corn if you use frozen—this is eventually going to hang out in the fridge for a while. Add black-eyed peas and stir until thoroughly mixed.

2   To prepare the dressing, in a small bowl, combine rice vinegar, balsamic vinegar, olive oil, water, garlic, cumin, chili powder and salt. Whisk together.

3   Pour dressing over bean mixture and stir to distribute evenly.

4   While this is delicious when served immediately, it's even better if you cover it and refrigerate for an hour or two or overnight. Season with salt and pepper before serving.

NUTRITION INFORMATION PER SERVING: 200 calories, 8 g total fat, 1 g saturated fat, 0 g trans fat, 0 mg cholesterol, 600 mg sodium, 28 g carbohydrate, 5 g fiber, 6 g sugar, 6 g protein, vitamin A 6%, vitamin C 60%, calcium 4%, iron 8%

pea points

To turn this salad into a meal, serve it on a bed of mixed greens and garnish it with crumbled tortilla chips and avocado for a taco salad, or pile it on top of a baked sweet potato for the ultimate stuffed potato.

Tortilla Soup

Makes 6 servings of approximately 1½ cups each

WHEN I FIRST MADE THIS SOUP, I HAD GRAND PLANS FOR CINCO DE MAYO.

There was going to be mariachi music. Maybe a piñata. Definitely, definitely margaritas. I prepped all my ingredients, put on a poncho and let the girls get out the maracas. Then I looked at the calendar. And promptly realized it was May 6. I missed it.

But I made my tortilla soup, anyway, and realized it was far too delicious to save for just one day of the year. Reader Jen agreed, saying, "I made this for dinner and it was a real hit with my husband! He was mmm-ing and saying over and over, 'This is so good!' We loved it and are definitely going to keep it in our regular rotation."

You do that, Jen. With some margaritas on the side.

INGREDIENTS

cooking spray or oil, to grease pot

1 medium yellow onion, chopped

1 large bell pepper, chopped

2 teaspoons garlic, minced

1 tablespoon cumin

1 14-ounce can diced tomatoes, in juice

1 14-ounce can black beans, drained and rinsed

1 4-ounce can green chiles, drained

1 quart vegetable broth

6 corn tortillas

sea salt to taste

salt and pepper to taste

1 lemon or lime wedge

diced avocado, organic cheddar cheese or nondairy cheddar cheese, organic sour cream or nondairy sour cream, sliced olives, halved cherry tomatoes, minced fresh cilantro, to garnish

DIRECTIONS

1   In a large pot that has been greased with cooking spray or oil, sauté onions and peppers over medium-high heat for 3 to 4 minutes. Add garlic and cumin and sauté for an additional minute, or until aromatic.

130

more peas, thank you

2 Add tomatoes, beans, chiles and vegetable broth and bring to boil. Lower heat and simmer for 15 to 20 minutes.

3 To prepare tortilla strips, preheat oven to 350 degrees F. Slice corn tortillas into thin, long strips and place on a baking sheet that has been greased with cooking spray or oil. Spray strips with a little more spray or oil and top with sea salt. Bake for 6 to 7 minutes on each side, or until crisp.

4 Season soup to taste with salt and pepper and add a squeeze of lemon or lime juice.

5 Ladle soup into bowls, garnish each bowl with tortilla strips and desired toppings and serve.

NUTRITION INFORMATION PER SERVING: 160 calories, 1 g total fat, 0 g saturated fat, 0 g trans fat, 0 mg cholesterol, 800 mg sodium, 33 g carbohydrate, 6 g fiber, 6 g sugar, 6 g protein, vitamin A 8%, vitamin C 50%, calcium 10%, iron 10%

Toppings not included in analysis.

pea points

The more you can get your family involved in building their own meals, the more they'll take pride in what they are eating. We love to ladle up bowls of this soup and then place all the toppings on a lazy Susan so we can create our own masterpieces right at the table.

Soups, Salads and Sandwiches

Chickpea Melts

Makes 8 open-faced sandwiches

WE DIDN'T EAT A LOT OF FISH IN MY HOUSE GROWING UP.

My dad loved seafood, but my mom, the house cook, despised it, so despite her love for him, we rarely ate it. That's why we don't eat a lot of parsnips or persimmons around here. Though I guess those are probably easier to work around.

So growing up, you'd never catch my mom serving up tuna melts. Who wants to melt fish and then eat it? Not my mom. Heck, probably not even my dad, although when he got in the kitchen, all bets were off, though he was stellar at his "world's biggest pancake" attempts.

But in theory, the tuna melt, as awful sounding as it is linguistically, isn't a bad idea. And my mom did fix a pretty mean tuna fish sandwich on occasion. Her rationale was, "If you put enough pickles in anything, you can make it edible." Preach on, Mama.

I like to think that this sandwich is a friendlier incarnation of the tuna melt. Melted chickpeas don't sound half bad. And even if you don't like chickpeas, if you put enough pickles in anything, you can make it edible. Except parsnips and persimmons.

INGREDIENTS

2 14-ounce cans chickpeas, drained and rinsed

4 large kosher dill pickles, chopped

4 celery stalks, chopped

1 cup fresh parsley, minced

2 tablespoons Dijon or yellow mustard

½ cup nondairy mayonnaise (i.e., Vegenaise) or organic mayonnaise

salt and pepper to taste

8 slices whole-grain bread

2 medium tomatoes, sliced

1 cup shredded nondairy cheddar cheese (i.e., Daiya) or organic cheddar cheese

DIRECTIONS

1 Preheat broiler.

2 Put chickpeas in a large bowl and smash with the backside of a fork until you've reached a chunky consistency. Add pickles, celery, parsley, mustard and mayo and combine well. Season with salt and pepper to taste.

3 Lightly toast bread in a toaster or toaster oven. Remove and top each slice with the chickpea mixture, two slices of tomato and 2 tablespoons shredded cheese.

4 Arrange open-faced sandwiches on a cookie sheet and place under the broiler for 2 to 3 minutes, or until cheese is melted and bubbly. Serve at once.

NUTRITION INFORMATION PER SERVING: 370 calories, 18 g total fat, 5 g saturated fat, 0 g trans fat, 25 mg cholesterol, 1570 mg sodium, 41 g carbohydrate, 8 g fiber, 8 g sugar, 5 g protein, vitamin A 25%, vitamin C 35%, calcium 20%, iron 20%

pea points

You can create many variations of this sandwich by changing the kind of beans and cheese you use. Try cannellini beans with mozzarella or pinto beans with pepper jack. You can even omit the mayo if you aren't a fan and sub in a mashed, ripe avocado. And the filling stuffed in whole wheat pitas is perfect for lunch boxes.

Soups, Salads and Sandwiches

Sunshine Kale Salad

Makes 2 large or 4 small servings

IT'S NOT ALWAYS EASY BEING A HEALTHY FOOD BLOGGER.

While other food bloggers can simply toss some bacon, some cake batter or a five-inch tower of frosting onto their creations—and often all three—I don't have that luxury.

I have to win hearts with quinoa.

With chia seeds.

With kale.

But sometimes my readers surprise me. Not to say that I haven't made many friends via peanut butter chocolate chip cookie dough balls. But among my most popular recipes is a humble kale salad.

It's made believers out of kale doubters.

Doubters like my dear friend Katie, who says, "I could live off this salad. It's all I need in life."

She adds, "Well, this salad and coconut cream pie."

I'll take it.

INGREDIENTS

1 head Italian kale (also known as Tuscan or dinosaur kale)

1 tablespoon tahini

2 tablespoons water

juice of 1 lemon

½ teaspoon chili powder

1 to 2 teaspoons garlic, minced

1 tablespoon nutritional yeast (optional)

salt and pepper to taste

pinch of sugar or stevia

DIRECTIONS

1   Wash kale and pat dry. Using a sharp knife, cut along each side of the kale stem, removing the thickest part of the stem.

2   Gather kale leaves into a bundle and cut across in 1–2-inch-wide strips and place in a large bowl.

3   For dressing, whisk together tahini, water, lemon juice, chili powder, garlic, nutritional yeast, salt and pepper and sugar or stevia. Adjust seasoning to taste.

4   Pour dressing over kale and massage dressing into leaves with clean hands.

5   Refrigerate, allowing dressing to soften kale for at least five minutes before serving.

NUTRITION INFORMATION PER SERVING: 60 calories, 2.5 g total fat, 0 g saturated fat, 0 g trans fat, 0 mg cholesterol, 30 mg sodium, 8 g carbohydrate, 2 g fiber, 0 g sugar, 4 g protein, vitamin A 160%, vitamin C 100%, calcium 8%, iron 6%

Based on 4 servings per recipe. Optional ingredients and toppings not included in analysis.

Dinners

Italian-Style Meatless
Meatball Subs 138

Kung Pao Tofu 141

Just Like Mom's
Meatless Meat Loaf 144

Zucchini
Quinoa Lasagna 147

Maple Dijon Tofu
Chops 150

Tofu Stuffin' Muffins 152

Mexican Millet Burgers 155

One Pan Roasted Sweet
Potato and Black Bean
Enchiladas 158

Spinach Artichoke
Calzones 161

Tempeh Tamale Pie 164

Tempeh Stroganoff 167

Roasted Chickpea
Tacos 170

Portabella
Mushroom Fajitas 173

Sloppy Josephines 175

Chickpeas
and Dumplings 177

Black-Eyed Pea
Veggie Burgers 180

Black Bean Dal 182

Italian-Style
Meatless Meatball Subs

Serves 4
This recipe was inspired by those infamous Subway meatball subs.

PEA DADDY AND I LIKE TO KEEP OUR MARRIAGE EXCITING.

So we have this fun little game we play called "Guess What Disgusting Thing I Used to Eat?" Let the sparks fly. It's not that we were intentionally trying to fill our bodies with nutritionally devoid food-like substances. It's just that we didn't know any better.

"I used to eat bologna sandwiches, and I'd butter the bread *and* put mayonnaise and cheese on it!"

"I would go to the grocery store bakery at lunch and eat a whole loaf of deli French bread by myself!"

"I'd eat a box of Red Vines and a mini-bag of Cheetos on my lunch break every day!"

"I'd go to McDonald's and get a Number Two Value Meal and eat the whole thing!"

That was me. Okay, those all were me. And for the record, a Number Two Value Meal is two cheeseburgers, a large fry and a large drink.

We were athletes, we were teenagers and we were stupid. I remember feeling pretty disappointed when I made the leap from high school basketball to college basketball and got a coach who actually understood a thing about nutrition. Turns out what you eat can either enhance or hinder your athletic performance. Who knew?

So after every away game, we'd pile into the bus, drive right by our old road trip favorites on fast-food row and head straight for our only choice: Subway. Hey, if it's good enough for Jared, it's good enough for me. (Isn't it interesting how we now know Jared on a one-name basis? He's like Madonna. Or Beyoncé. But just with the somewhat dubious distinction that he'd eat submarine sandwiches all day, every day, for weeks on end.) Of course, I, being the food rebel that I have always been, would find a way to get one of the most unhealthful things on the Subway menu—the meatball sub.

"Oh, yeah, Pea Daddy, I used to eat an entire meatball sub with extra cheese! Sometimes I'd even get a twelve-inch!"

I win.

Yet I've found a way to make the infamous sandwich of basketball road trip days of yore a really satisfying, delicious and healthy meal. With a toasty bun, "meaty" bean balls, a classic sauce and cheese, I think even Jared himself would be into this one. Morning, noon or night.

INGREDIENTS

2 tablespoons flaxseeds
(or approximately
3 tablespoons ground)

½ cup old-fashioned oats

1 14-ounce can pinto beans,
drained and rinsed

¼ cup yellow onion, chopped

½ teaspoon garlic, minced

2 teaspoons organic
Worcestershire sauce

1 teaspoon olive oil

1 tablespoon nutritional yeast

½ teaspoon dried oregano

½ teaspoon dried parsley

¼ teaspoon salt

pepper to taste

4 whole wheat hot dog buns or
hoagie rolls, split and toasted

cooking spray, to grease cookie
sheet

2 cups organic spaghetti sauce

¾ cup shredded nondairy
mozzarella cheese (i.e., Daiya)
or organic mozzarella cheese

1 5-ounce can sliced black olives,
drained

chiffonade of fresh basil,
to garnish (optional)

DIRECTIONS

1   Preheat oven to 375 degrees F.

2   In a high-speed blender or food processor, process flaxseeds and
    oats until finely ground. Add beans, onion, garlic, Worcestershire
    sauce, oil, nutritional yeast, oregano, parsley, salt and pepper.

3   Pulse blender or food processor until all the ingredients are
    combined, but not so much that a paste forms.

4   Using a spoon or a mini-scoop, scoop bean mixture and roll into
    golf ball–size balls. Place on a cookie sheet that has been sprayed
    with cooking spray. Bake balls for 20 to 22 minutes, rotating at least
    once during baking.

5   Place baked "meatballs" on toasted buns or rolls and top each with
    ¼ to ½ cup spaghetti sauce, 3 tablespoons of cheese, a sprinkling
    of olives and basil, if using.

pea points

Make smaller
"meatballs" and
serve these over
spaghetti for
another family
favorite.

NUTRITION INFORMATION PER SERVING: 940 calories, 36 g total fat, 8 g saturated fat,
0 g trans fat, 10 mg cholesterol, 3110 mg sodium, 133 g carbohydrate, 27 g fiber, 48 g sugar,
26 g protein, vitamin A 60%, vitamin C 100%, calcium 25%, iron 20%

Optional ingredients and toppings not included in analysis.

more peas, thank you

Kung Pao Tofu

Serves 4
This recipe was inspired by that takeout classic, Kung Pao chicken.

I ALWAYS THOUGHT I WOULD BE A WAITRESS WHEN I GREW UP.

It runs in the family. My mom and grandma were waitresses at a local Chinese restaurant. It's literally a hole-in-the-wall. It is not in the nicest part of a town, has only about fifteen small tables, and in the old days the owners, their close relatives, my grandmother and my mom were the only employees. Thirty years later, it's still in business. And it still has the best Chinese food in town. Present company excluded, of course.

I wanted to be just like my mom. My hair done up tight and away from my face and a Bic pen behind my ear. My nails and lips painted red. A black, faded apron tied around my waist, the pockets jingling when I walked away from those hasty customers who threw whatever spare change they had on the table for tips. The change would end up in a white ceramic pitcher on my mom's dresser, along with the random paper clip, an earring missing its mate and a gold token, whose very existence gave me unending hope that we'd wind up back at Chuck E. Cheese's someday.

My mom would bring us into the restaurant to visit, and the owners, Sean and Teresa, doted on my brother and me. They'd let us play with the cash register until the insistent buzzing of the error messages drove the customers crazy. From the front counter, we'd watch my mom and my grandma rush about the restaurant, topping off water glasses, wiping up drips of sweet 'n' sour sauce from the tabletops and refilling soy sauce carafes. We could hear the chorus of foreign voices from the kitchen, hear the hiss of chilled vegetables and meat hitting the hot wok and the clang of spatulas dancing in the pan.

We could have sat there forever, but eventually, my mom's shift would be up, and Sean and Teresa would send each of us home with a free pack of gum from the front counter display.

But, of course, we'd have to eat dinner first. Egg flower soup. Beef and broccoli. Noodle salad. Fried wontons. Barbecued pork. Kung Pao chicken. All washed down with five sticks of Juicy Fruit. My jaw still aches just thinking about it.

I didn't become a waitress. I don't have a pen behind my ear or red painted nails, and though my pockets are full, it's only because I've been assigned the task of carrying Lulu's rock collection. Still, I can't help but get excited when I heat up the wok and hear the hiss of vegetables hitting the hot surface. It makes me happy to share my Kung Pao with you.

And there's Juicy Fruit for dessert.

INGREDIENTS

5 tablespoons soy sauce

1 teaspoon mirin

¼ cup water

1 15-ounce package extra-firm tofu, drained, pressed and cut into 2 x 2-inch squares

½ cup vegetable broth

¼ cup balsamic vinegar

1 tablespoon cornstarch

2 teaspoons agave nectar

1 teaspoon sesame oil

cooking spray or oil, to grease baking sheet

5 small dried red chiles, halved and seeded (optional)

1 large red bell pepper, chopped

3 green onions, chopped

1 tablespoon fresh ginger, minced

1 tablespoon garlic, minced

2 cups cooked brown rice

¼ cup roasted peanuts

DIRECTIONS

1   In a large bowl combine 3 tablespoons of the soy sauce, mirin and 2 tablespoons of the water. Carefully add tofu and stir until lightly coated. Refrigerate and marinate anywhere from 30 minutes to overnight.

2   In a small bowl, combine broth, vinegar, remaining soy sauce, remaining water, cornstarch, agave nectar and sesame oil. Set aside.

3   Preheat broiler. Place tofu cubes on a baking sheet that has been lightly oiled or sprayed with cooking spray. Broil tofu for 10 to 12 minutes, flipping once during cooking, or until tofu has started to brown and crisp around the edges.

4   Place a large skillet or wok that has been lightly oiled or sprayed with cooking spray over medium-high heat. Add chiles, red pepper, green onions and ginger and sauté for 4 to 5 minutes, or until pepper begins to soften. Add garlic and sauté for about 30 seconds. Pour in sauce mixture and cook until sauce thickens, about 1 minute. Add tofu and stir to coat. Serve tofu over rice and top each serving with 1 tablespoon roasted peanuts.

NUTRITION INFORMATION PER SERVING: 330 calories, 12 g total fat, 1 g saturated fat, 0 g trans fat, 0 mg cholesterol, 810 mg sodium, 42 g carbohydrate, 4 g fiber, 9 g sugar, 17 g protein, vitamin A 25%, vitamin C 130%, calcium 15%, iron 25%

Optional ingredients not included in analysis.

Just Like Mom's
Meatless Meat Loaf

Makes 1 standard loaf, serves 6
This recipe was inspired by my mom's classic meat loaf. I think Chad would
like that, too.

WE HAVE A LITMUS TEST WHENEVER IT COMES TO NEW RECIPES.

We call it the Chad Test. It's named for our friend Chad, who is about as big a meat eater as they come. In fact, the Chad Test is merely hypothetical, because I don't think there's any chance he would eat anything that comes out of my kitchen, solely based on principle.

I'm convinced Chad takes vacations to Disneyland just so he can get the turkey leg on a stick. Or maybe it's just so he can text Pea Daddy a picture of a turkey leg on a stick. He once suggested that I dress as a piece of bacon for Halloween. He drove home his point with a little Photoshop work, and thus I became Mama Bacon.

It's safe to say that the signed copy of our cookbook that I gave to Chad is now being used to keep his balcony window open as he grills steaks in violation of his building code. So whenever we have an especially satisfying meal, something hearty, even "meaty," Pea Daddy always pipes up, saying, "You could feed this to Chad and he wouldn't know the difference."

I'm wondering if Pea Daddy has ever met Chad. But even if Chad could tell the difference between this and his mom's meat loaf, that doesn't mean he wouldn't like it. Or that you wouldn't. Because for me at least, the thing I loved about meat loaf was the cozy smell of the spices filling the house. The big slab on my plate, next to a pile of mashed potatoes. And the best part—the thick, ketchupy crust that formed on the top, which I always saved for the last few perfect bites.

In other words, this may not pass for meat loaf exactly, but it would totally pass the Chad Test. Trust me. Mama Bacon knows these things.

INGREDIENTS

3 cups cooked lentils or black beans, drained and rinsed

¾ cup old-fashioned oats, ground to a fine flour

⅓ cup yellow onion, chopped

1½ teaspoons garlic, minced

¼ teaspoon ground ginger

1 teaspoon Italian seasoning

1 tablespoon ground flaxseed

1 tablespoon vegan Worcestershire sauce

1 tablespoon soy sauce

1 teaspoon Dijon mustard

salt and pepper to taste

cooking spray or oil, to grease loaf pan

Topping:
⅔ cup organic ketchup

¼ cup light brown sugar

2 teaspoons Dijon mustard

½ teaspoon liquid smoke (optional)

DIRECTIONS

1   Preheat oven to 400 degrees F.

2   In a blender or food processor, combine 2 cups of the lentils or beans, ground oats, onion, garlic, ginger, Italian seasoning, ground flaxseed, Worcestershire sauce, soy sauce, mustard and salt and pepper. Pulse until the mixture comes together, but do not overmix.

3   Transfer lentil-oat mixture to a large bowl and stir in remaining lentils.

4   Place lentil-oat mixture in a loaf pan that has been sprayed with cooking spray or lightly greased with oil.

5   To prepare the topping in a small bowl, combine ketchup, brown sugar, mustard and liquid smoke, if using. Spread ketchup mixture over lentil-oat loaf.

6   Bake for 25 to 30 minutes, or until the edges are crisp and the center has set. Let cool almost entirely before cutting.

pea points

You know what leftover meat loaf is good for, right? Serve a slab of this on some whole-grain bread with a smear of nondairy mayo or, better yet, an Mmmm Sauce (pp. 83–89) and you'll be in leftover heaven.

NUTRITION INFORMATION PER SERVING: 230 calories, 1.5 g total fat, 0 g saturated fat, 0 g trans fat, 0 mg cholesterol, 930 mg sodium, 45 g carbohydrate, 10 g fiber, 16 g sugar, 10 g protein, vitamin A 6%, vitamin C 15%, calcium 6%, iron 15%

Optional ingredients not included in analysis.

Zucchini Quinoa Lasagna

Makes 6 servings

NECESSITY IS THE MOTHER OF INVENTION.

And trust me, I have needs. I needed to get rid of a lot of zucchini in the summer. A lot a lot. Turns out if you don't pick zucchini for several months, they get to be the size of a baby and you need an epidural to be able to carry them inside your house. Or a glass of red wine. Whatever is handier.

I also needed to find a way to put together a lasagna that didn't require buying packaged noodles, trying not to break them while putting them in boiling water, trying not to break them while removing them from boiling water and trying not to break them while layering them in a massive casserole dish. Stupid noodles.

One more need: finding a recipe stellar enough to be featured in *Vegetarian Times* magazine. Necessity is the mother of invention. And I am the mother of Zucchini Quinoa Lasagna. But I'm not the only mother to appreciate the deliciousness of this dish. Reader Roberta says, "I almost always have a spare one of these lasagnas in the freezer for unexpected dinner guests. Everyone always asks for the recipe! My guilty secret is that I always make extra of the quinoa filling so I can snack on it while the lasagna cooks!"

It's okay, Roberta. No one needs to know. But we all need this lasagna.

INGREDIENTS

2 large zucchini

1 to 2 teaspoons salt

1 cup quinoa, rinsed

2 cups vegetable broth

½ cup tomato sauce

¼ cup yellow onion, minced

1 teaspoon dried oregano

¼ cup fresh basil, minced

¼ cup fresh parsley, minced

2 tablespoons nondairy or organic cream cheese

salt and pepper to taste

1 14-ounce jar organic marinara sauce

½ cup shredded nondairy mozzarella cheese (i.e., Daiya) or organic mozzarella cheese (optional)

DIRECTIONS

1   Preheat oven to 400 degrees F.

2   To prepare zucchini, cut a strip off of one side to make a flat base. Then slice zucchini into "noodles." You want 12 noodles in total, so each slice should be about ¼ inch thick.

3   Place noodles in a colander and sprinkle with salt. Layer noodles between paper towels. Let them sit and absorb moisture while you prepare the quinoa.

4   Combine quinoa, vegetable broth, tomato sauce, onion and oregano in a large saucepan and bring to a boil. Cover, lower heat and simmer for 20 minutes.

5   When quinoa has absorbed all the liquid, fold in basil, parsley and cream cheese. Add salt and pepper to taste.

6   Pour enough marinara sauce in an 8 x 8-inch baking dish to cover the bottom.

7   Using a clean, dry towel, blot remaining moisture and salt from zucchini and layer 4 noodles across the sauce.

8   Spread a layer of quinoa on the zucchini, and cover with ⅓ cup marinara sauce. Repeat with another layer of zucchini, quinoa and sauce.

9   Add the final layer of zucchini and top with remaining sauce and cheese, if using.

10 Bake lasagna for 30 minutes, or until heated through and zucchini is tender.

NUTRITION INFORMATION PER SERVING: 200 calories, 6 g total fat, 1.5 g saturated fat, 0 g trans fat, 0 mg cholesterol, 1020 mg sodium, 31 g carbohydrate, 4 g fiber, 11 g sugar, 9 g protein, vitamin A 30%, vitamin C 35%, calcium 15%, iron 20%

Optional ingredients not included in analysis.

Maple Dijon Tofu Chops

Serves 4

This recipe was inspired by 1970s sitcoms and our geeky nostalgia for pork chops and applesauce.

I'M NOT PROUD OF THE AMOUNT OF *BRADY BUNCH* KNOWLEDGE I HAVE FLOATING AROUND IN THIS BIG OLD HEAD OF MINE.

I'm even less proud of the amount of *Brady Bunch* knowledge Pea Daddy has floating around in that normal-size head of his. We can tell you exactly which episode has the great card house building competition and whose bracelet dooms the whole thing, we can tell you why volcanos and the booster club don't mix, and we can tell you how the tables get turned on that bully who teases Cindy about her lisp. Like I "thaid," I'm not proud. I *am* proud that we can all sit down to a meal that reminds us of Peter's famed favorite, "pork chops and applesauce." Here's a story, of a lovely dinner....

INGREDIENTS

⅓ cup maple syrup

¼ cup Dijon mustard

¼ cup apple juice

½ teaspoon allspice

1 teaspoon cumin

½ teaspoon salt (preferably smoked sea salt)

1 15-ounce package extra-firm tofu, drained, pressed and cut into 2 x 3-inch slabs

parchment paper, lightly greased or sprayed with cooking spray

2 cups unsweetened applesauce

DIRECTIONS

1   In a large shallow bowl, combine maple syrup, mustard, apple juice, allspice, cumin and salt. Place tofu slabs in marinade, turning to coat. Allow tofu to rest anywhere from 30 minutes to overnight.

2   Preheat broiler.

3   Line a cookie sheet with parchment paper that has been lightly greased or sprayed with cooking spray. Place tofu on cookie sheet.

more peas, thank you

4   Broil tofu for 10 to 12 minutes, turning once during cooking.

5   Serve at once with applesauce.

NUTRITION INFORMATION PER SERVING: 140 calories, 2.5 g total fat, 0 g saturated fat, 0 g trans fat, 0 mg cholesterol, 660 mg sodium, 24 g carbohydrate, 0 g fiber, 18 g sugar, 5 g protein, vitamin A 0%, vitamin C 8%, calcium 8%, iron 10%

Tofu Stuffin' Muffins

Makes 9 muffins, serves 4

"BUT WAIT!" YOU SAY.

"Stuffing is not an entrée! It's a side dish." You are wrong, my friend. Sometimes it's not even that. One of the worst Thanksgivings I ever had had absolutely not a stitch of stuffing. There's no deeper meaning to this story. It wasn't that I followed my boyfriend to his family's house for dinner and that, for some unknown reason, not only didn't they teach their son that framed pictures of oneself are not suitable birthday gifts after three years of dating, but they also didn't serve stuffing. And then I learned the important life lesson that you never choose a cute boy over family.

No, the actual worst Thanksgiving was crummy simply because I didn't get any stuffing. That's not to say that there wasn't any stuffing. My grandma had gone to great lengths to make sure that even though there was just a cup or two of carbtastic deliciousness stuffed in the bird, there was also an entire six-pound casserole dish baked up on the side. We were going to get our stuffing *on* this year.

more peas, thank you

Unfortunately, so was Bunny. Bunny was my grandparents' eleven-year-old, sweet-natured miniature schnauzer who had an undying love for people food. And I do mean undying. She was especially interested in holiday-themed people food, as we learned one Easter, when she unwrapped and ate an entire bag of pretty pink and green pastel foiled Hershey's kisses on Easter morning. See what I mean by undying? Grandpa had a glittery yard for a week, but Bunny survived.

The Thanksgiving Without Stuffing started like any other Thanksgiving. My mom and aunt were fighting over the turkey, my dad was tablescaping the place settings like he was Martha Stewart, and Grandma was setting out the side dishes on the table in the formal dining room, while the rest of us watched football and talked without actually listening to each other in the living room.

When the last timer had gone off on the oven, the carving knife had been brought out and people had been corralled out of the living room, we heard my grandmother's nasally voice piercing through the clatter and chatter.

"Ohhhhhh my gawwwwwwwd!"

We walked into the dining room to see Bunny on the dining room table, her whiskers full of stuffing, her belly distended beyond anything I've ever seen outside of my third trimester, and a completely empty casserole dish of, you guessed it, stuffing. It took three men to lift that dog off the table and the entire evening we feared she might in fact actually explode. She was stuffed.

Being the giver I am, I relinquished my two tablespoons of stuffing from the bird, and thus my Thanksgiving was joyless and empty. Never again. In fact, now I give stuffing a central role. This version has all the flavor of my grandma's dish, but is grain free and protein packed. It's meaty enough to serve as a main dish and the only thing you need to stuff it in is your face.

Pea Kitty better keep her paws off.

INGREDIENTS

cooking spray, to grease skillet and muffin tin

1 small yellow onion, diced

2 celery stalks, diced

3 tablespoons fresh parsley, minced

1 tablespoon fresh rosemary, minced

1 tablespoon fresh thyme, minced

1 tablespoon fresh sage, minced

1 15-ounce package extra-firm tofu, drained, patted dry and crumbled

2 teaspoons garlic, minced

1 tablespoon nutritional yeast

3 tablespoons soy sauce

1 organic egg or 2 flaxseed "eggs" (¼ cup water + 2 tablespoons ground flaxseed)

salt and pepper to taste

DIRECTIONS

1 Preheat oven to 400 degrees F. In a large skillet coated with cooking spray, sauté onion, celery, parsley, rosemary, thyme and sage over medium heat for 4 to 5 minutes, or until softened and aromatic.

2 Place tofu, garlic, nutritional yeast, soy sauce and egg or "eggs" in a blender or food processor and pulse until crumbly and combined.

3 Add tofu mixture to skillet and stir so vegetables are fully incorporated. Add salt and pepper to taste.

4 Scoop tofu stuffing into 9 cups in a muffin tin that has been sprayed with cooking spray. Bake for 25 to 30 minutes, or until muffins are firm and browned. Let cool before removing from pan.

NUTRITION INFORMATION PER SERVING: 45 calories, 2 g total fat, 0 g saturated fat, 0 g trans fat, 25 mg cholesterol, 200 mg sodium, 3 g carbohydrate, <1 g fiber, 1 g sugar, 4 g protein, vitamin A 4%, vitamin C 6%, calcium 4%, iron 6%

more peas, thank you

Mexican Millet Burgers

Makes 4 large patties

PEA DADDY AND I HAVE A GROOVY KIND OF LOVE.

He is the best man I know. And since he is the best man I know, I like to do nice things for him sometimes. Sometimes this means matching up and stacking each of his pairs of identical tube socks meticulously in his drawer and never, ever folding them into balls, because that would stretch them out. Pea Daddy hates slouchy socks. But luckily, not slouchy wives.

Sometimes I do other nice things, like bring the garbage cans in from the curb and put them nicely at the side of the house where they belong. Well, truthfully, it's my dad that does that. He comes to visit on Fridays usually, and that's trash day. I did put the cans away once, but only because I saw my dad do it. Maybe he's the best man I know.

The most frequent way I do nice things for Pea Daddy is through food. I'm not really the type of wife that says, "Look! I made your favorite!" because due to my profession, it's rare that we eat the same thing twice. "You like my new recipe? Good. I'll write it up and then we'll never have it again." But I like to give him choices. I'll send an email in the late afternoon that says, "No, I don't want to buy a Groupon for facial waxing, so stop forwarding them to me." I'm so romantic that way. But then I'll tack on, "P.S. What do you want for dinner? Burgers or burritos?"

Pea Daddy knows full well that I've probably already made cookies or brownies or smoothies or dough balls for the blog that day, and thus he's being given the option of two things that require me only to a) open the freezer and defrost a patty (yes, it happens to us all) or b) open a can of beans. He knows, and yet he takes a chance, asking for what he wants in the most passive-aggressive way possible. He should be a mother in his next life.

"I know we've both worked hard all day, but boy, one of your homemade veggie burgers would taste so good right now. They're just the best."

So I leave his socks unfolded. I leave the cans out by the curb. (Dad will get them Friday.) And I make a homemade veggie burger for the best man I know.

He says, "Thank you." He says, "I love you." He says, "Mmmm."

And it works. Groovy.

INGREDIENTS

1 organic egg or flaxseed "egg" (3 tablespoons water + 1 tablespoon ground flaxseed)

1½ cups warm water

1½ cups millet

cooking spray or oil, to grease skillet

½ cup yellow onion, chopped

1 teaspoon garlic, minced

½ cup carrots, finely chopped or grated

1 14-ounce can garbanzo beans, drained, rinsed and roughly pureed

¼ cup fresh cilantro, finely minced

1 tablespoon extra-virgin olive oil

1 tablespoon soy sauce

1½ teaspoons cumin

1 teaspoon chili powder

salt and pepper to taste

DIRECTIONS

1 Preheat oven to 350 degrees F.

2 Combine flaxseed and water in a small bowl and set aside.

3 Prepare millet by grinding 1 cup of it into a flour in a blender, food processor or coffee/spice grinder.

4 Bring 1½ cups water to a boil. Add remaining ½ cup millet, cover and reduce heat. Simmer for 15 minutes. Remove from heat and allow millet to sit for 5 minutes before fluffing with a fork.

5 In a large skillet lightly coated with cooking spray or oil, sauté onion, garlic and carrots over medium-high heat until tender, about 5 minutes.

6 In a large bowl, combine organic egg or flaxseed "egg," ground millet, cooked millet, onion mixture, garbanzo beans, cilantro, olive oil, soy sauce, cumin and chili powder. Add salt and pepper to taste.

pea points

These burgers scream for nontraditional toppings, like salsa, Almost Chipotle Guacamole (p. 96) and Nacho Mmmm Sauce (p. 86). The messier the better!

7 Form burger mixture into patties, packing tightly.

8 Bake for 25 to 30 minutes, turning once, or until golden and crisp.

9 Serve on toasted buns and top with the trimmings of your choice.

NUTRITION INFORMATION PER SERVING: 490 calories, 10 g total fat, 1.5 g saturated fat, 0 g trans fat, 0 mg cholesterol, 460 mg sodium, 84 g carbohydrate, 13 g fiber, 2 g sugar, 15 g protein, vitamin A 60%, vitamin C 10%, calcium 4%, iron 20%

One Pan Roasted Sweet Potato and Black Bean Enchiladas

Makes 10 enchiladas

DON'T SKIP OVER THIS RECIPE BECAUSE YOU THINK YOU DON'T WANT TO GO TO ALL THE TROUBLE TO MAKE ENCHILADAS.

You don't want to cook up the filling in a skillet. You don't want to simmer the sauce in a pot. You don't want to then layer everything in a casserole dish and bake it. Guess what? I don't want to, either.

Fortunately, I have made my life all about getting a lot of things done, and done well, with as little effort as possible. I sleep in my gym clothes. Sports bras and shorts with built-in underwear and key pockets are not sexy. But I never miss a workout. I wear the same mascara for at least two days in a row. And I get pinkeye once every six months. I unpack Gigi's lunch box, salvage what I can for the next day and then repack it all at once. Sometimes this means she gets the same I Love You napkin two days in a row. And the same slightly white baby carrots. Funny, I never have to repack the cookies.

This practicality/laziness is not only accepted, but also appreciated by my husband. I remember when Pea Daddy and I started dating, there was always a bowl and spoon on the edge of his sink, no matter what. I'd come over to watch a movie—bowl and spoon on the sink. I'd swing by to drop off a contracts outline—bowl and spoon on the sink. I'd accept his dinner invite and he'd get clean dishes out of the cupboard for us to eat off of, but—bowl and spoon on the sink. Finally one day, I got up the nerve to ask him why there was always a bowl and a spoon on the edge of his sink.

"Oh, that's my cereal bowl and spoon."

Come again?

"I just rinse the bowl out each morning after breakfast and sit it there for the next morning. No use in washing it when I'm just going to use it again."

Wow. That's a whole new level of both laziness and grossness. Needless to say, all of our breakfast dishes get washed daily in our house. But if I can save a few dishes and a whole lot of effort by making an incredible batch of enchiladas in one pan? That's just genius.

Try it. You'll see. And if you want to sleep in your mascara, you have my blessing. And probably pinkeye.

INGREDIENTS

Filling:
cooking spray or oil, to grease casserole dish

5 medium sweet potatoes, peeled and diced (3 cups)

1 medium yellow onion, diced

1 15-ounce can fire-roasted diced tomatoes, drained

2 cups prepared organic salsa (i.e., Fire-Roasted Salsa in a Cinch from *Peas and Thank You*)

2 teaspoons garlic, minced

1 15-ounce can black beans, drained and rinsed

Sauce:
1 15-ounce can tomato sauce

1½ cups vegetable broth

1 tablespoon chili powder

1 teaspoon garlic powder

1 teaspoon onion powder

1 teaspoon dried oregano

salt and pepper to taste

Enchiladas:
10 corn tortillas, warmed

½ cup shredded nondairy cheddar cheese (i.e., Daiya) or organic cheddar cheese

Almost Chipotle Guacamole (p. 96), sliced black olives, minced fresh cilantro, to garnish (optional)

159

Dinners

DIRECTIONS

1 Preheat oven to 450 degrees F.

2 Lightly grease a 13 x 9-inch casserole dish with cooking spray or oil. Place sweet potatoes in the casserole dish and roast for 10 minutes. Stir, add onions to the dish and return to the oven for another 10 minutes.

3 While sweet potatoes and onions are roasting, whisk together tomato sauce, broth, chili powder, garlic powder, onion powder and oregano. Season with salt and pepper to taste.

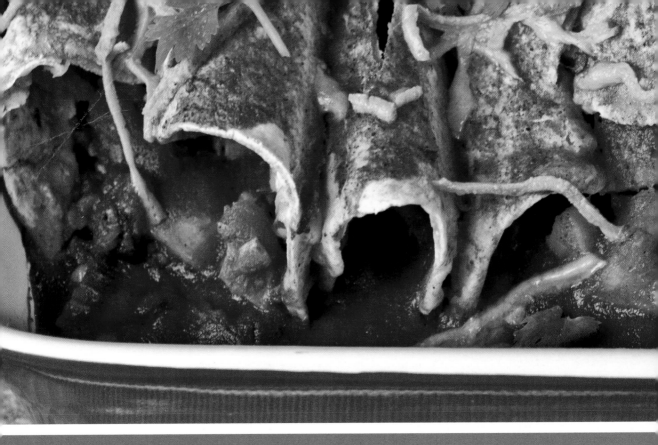

4   Remove sweet potatoes and onions from the casserole dish and place in a large bowl. Add tomatoes, salsa, garlic and black beans, and mash all filling ingredients together with a potato masher until well combined.

5   Reduce oven temperature to 350 degrees F.

6   Pour 1 cup of the sauce in the bottom of the casserole dish. Fill tortillas with filling, roll and pack together, seam side down, in the casserole dish. Top with remaining sauce and cheese. Bake for 25 to 30 minutes, or until cheese is melted and sauce is bubbly. Garnish with guacamole, olives and cilantro, if desired.

NUTRITION INFORMATION PER SERVING: 180 calories, 3.5 g total fat, 1.5 g saturated fat, 0 g trans fat, 0 mg cholesterol, 750 mg sodium, 32 g carbohydrate, 5 g fiber, 4 g sugar, 6 g protein, vitamin A 10%, vitamin C 15%, calcium 10%, iron 10%

Optional ingredients and toppings not included in analysis.

Spinach Artichoke Calzones

Makes 4 large calzones

SPINACH ARTICHOKE DIP? GOOD.

Calzones? Good. Spinach artichoke calzones? Goooood. These calzones can be as easy or as hard as you want to make. Let me tell you exactly how hard I made them.

Calzones are one of Pea Daddy's favorite foods. There's a little Italian joint near his college where we'd go and get these massive calzones before going to basketball games. I knew I could get out of any doghouse if I could somehow find a way to re-create these amazing calzones. This doghouse came in the form of a pair of jeans I bought myself for Christmas. Twice. One color of wash is never enough. Unless you get the credit card statement.

I'd done all the prep work ahead of time. While the girls and I did some Christmas shopping (otherwise known as dragging them off the toy aisle for forty-five minutes so I can get a roll of Scotch tape), I proofed my own dough. I ran with the girls to mail some packages (otherwise known as dragging the girls off of the velvet-roped poles while I buy stamps), and then came home to make my own sauce. I was exhausted.

I'd just started to sauté my onions for the filling when I went to grab the spinach out of the fridge. No spinach. I checked the vegetable drawer. No spinach. I moved three jars of pickles. No spinach. I put a dollar in the Swear Jar and still no spinach. I didn't want to do it but I had to go get spinach. No way I was staying in that designer jean–covered doghouse. "Put on your coats, girls! Grab your shoes! Those are on the wrong feet! Yes, you can get a cookie from the bakery! But you have to give me a bite."

We finally made it to the store. I bought spinach. I came home, took off the shoes, took off the coats, wiped chocolate chip cookies from faces and sat my new bag of spinach on the counter. Right next to my old bag of spinach. I put another dollar in the Swear Jar.

Case in point, these calzones can be as easy or as hard as you want to make. I vote easy. But either way, they are totally worth it. Just like my jeans.

INGREDIENTS

cooking spray or oil, to grease skillet

1 cup yellow onion, chopped

5 cups organic baby spinach

1 14-ounce can artichoke hearts, drained and chopped into bite-size pieces

1 14-ounce can garbanzo beans, drained and rinsed

1 teaspoon garlic, minced

3 tablespoons nutritional yeast

2 teaspoons lemon juice

¼ cup nondairy milk (unsweetened, plain) or organic milk

1 teaspoon salt

½ teaspoon dried basil

1½ teaspoons Italian seasoning

1 16-ounce whole wheat pizza dough (store-bought or your favorite recipe)

1⅓ cups organic marinara sauce (store-bought or your favorite recipe)

DIRECTIONS

1   Preheat oven to 425 degrees F.

2   In a large skillet lightly coated with cooking spray or oil, sauté onion over medium to medium-high heat. Cook for 5 to 6 minutes, or until onion is tender and starts to brown.

3   Lower heat and add spinach and artichoke hearts. Cook until spinach is wilted, about 3 minutes.

4   In a food processor or high-speed blender, combine beans, garlic, nutritional yeast, lemon juice, milk, salt, basil and Italian seasoning. Pulse until relatively smooth.

5   Add bean mixture to skillet and stir until thoroughly combined.

6   Divide pizza dough into four small balls. Flatten balls into a large football shape. Place a large scoop of filling in the middle of each "football" and fold dough over, crimping edges. Repeat until all calzones are made.

pea points

The filling for these calzones also makes a great appetizer. Serve it with raw veggies or whole-grain crackers for a great spinach artichoke dip stand-in.

7 Lightly grease a baking sheet with cooking spray or oil and place calzones on it.

8 Bake for 15 to 20 minutes, or until calzones are golden brown on the bottom and around the edges.

9 Serve each calzone with ⅓ cup marinara sauce for dipping.

NUTRITION INFORMATION PER SERVING: 520 calories, 13 g total fat, 0 g saturated fat, 0 g trans fat, 0 mg cholesterol, 1650 mg sodium, 104 g carbohydrate, 12 g fiber, 10 g sugar, 19 g protein, vitamin A 80%, vitamin C 45%, calcium 15%, iron 20%

Tempeh Tamale Pie

Makes 6 servings of approximately 2 cups each

TEMPEH WAS A HARD SELL FOR ME WHEN IT CAME TO TRYING
STAND-INS FOR MEAT.

Of course, a good rule of thumb when trying anything new and rather
alien-looking is *not* to just open the package, break off a piece like it's
a Kit Kat bar and then pop it in your mouth. But once I learned how to
use tempeh and, more specifically, thought of grating it and using it as
a substitute for ground beef, the possibilities were endless.

This Tempeh Tamale Pie will make even the biggest tempeh skeptic
(you're looking at her) a fan. It's one of our site's most popular recipes,
a big feat for a dish that features an ingredient that most people think,
well, tastes like feet. Reader Maggie, a big fan, says, "This recipe is perfect!
This was the first time I had ever used tempeh, and it is delicious. Even
my husband loves it, and he was convinced that he only liked my ground
beef tamale pie. My four-year-old literally gobbled it up!"

That's all the convincing I need. Break me off a piece of that tamale pie.

INGREDIENTS

cooking spray or oil,
to grease skillet

1 medium yellow onion, chopped

1 8-ounce package tempeh,
crumbled

2 teaspoons garlic, minced

1 teaspoon chili powder

½ teaspoon salt

2 teaspoons apple cider vinegar
or red wine vinegar

1 teaspoon maple syrup plus
1 tablespoon

1 14-ounce can tomato sauce

1 15-ounce can pinto beans,
drained and rinsed

⅔ cup cornmeal

⅓ cup whole wheat pastry flour

2 teaspoons baking powder

¼ teaspoon salt

½ cup nondairy milk or
organic milk

2 tablespoons unsweetened
applesauce

1 cup frozen corn, defrosted and drained

1 6-ounce can of sliced black olives, drained (optional)

⅓ cup shredded nondairy cheddar cheese (i.e., Daiya) or organic cheddar cheese (optional)

½ cup nondairy or organic dairy sour cream (optional)

DIRECTIONS

1 Preheat oven to 400 degrees F.

2 Place a large skillet greased with cooking spray or oil over medium-high heat. Add onion and sauté until softened and starting to brown, about 4 to 5 minutes.

3 Add tempeh to the skillet with the sautéed onion. Cook tempeh, stirring frequently for 2 to 3 minutes, or until lightly brown.

4 To the skillet, add garlic, chili powder, salt, vinegar, 1 teaspoon maple syrup, tomato sauce and beans.

5 Allow tempeh-bean mixture to simmer for a few minutes to meld flavors. Transfer to a 2-quart baking dish that has been sprayed with cooking spray or lightly coated with oil and set aside.

6 In a medium bowl, combine cornmeal, flour, baking powder and salt.

7 In a small bowl, combine milk, 1 tablespoon maple syrup and applesauce.

8 Add wet ingredients to the cornmeal mixture and stir until just combined. Gently fold in the corn.

9 Spread corn mixture carefully and evenly over the top of the tempeh-bean mixture. If using, top the casserole with cheese.

10 Bake for 15 to 20 minutes, or until the cheese has melted and the crust has set and started to brown.

11 Serve with sliced olives and sour cream, if desired.

pea points

To make this recipe gluten free, make sure your tempeh is gluten free and sub millet, chickpea, oat or brown rice flour for the wheat flour. If you truly don't want to use tempeh, you can always sub in an extra can of pinto beans and this will still make a fantastic pie.

165

Dinners

NUTRITION INFORMATION PER SERVING: 310 calories, 5 g total fat, 0.5 g saturated fat, 0 g trans fat, 0 mg cholesterol, 840 mg sodium, 55 g carbohydrate, 10 g fiber, 11 g sugar, 15 g protein, vitamin A 25%, vitamin C 25%, calcium 10%, iron 20%

Optional ingredients and toppings not included in analysis.

Tempeh Stroganoff

Makes 4 servings

IT DIDN'T TAKE LONG TO FIGURE OUT WHO WAS GOING TO PLAY WHAT SPECIFIC ROLES IN OUR MARRIAGE.

The interest charges and late fees on my credit card statements meant Pea Daddy would handle the finances. Pea Daddy's revelation that hair shampoo and hair conditioner are two separate and completely different things meant that I would be doing the health and beauty product shopping. Pea Daddy's one failed attempt at making me dinner meant that I would do the cooking. Now and forever. Till death do us part.

My first clue that perhaps this was not going to be the finest meal of my life was when I walked into Pea Daddy's apartment and saw him boiling some sort of ground meat in an ancient electric skillet, stirring it with a fork. He had a stove. I assume he had a real frying pan. I also assume I ingested a great deal of lead coating that Pea Daddy was scraping off of the bottom of his great-grandmother's electric skillet. Yum!

After an unbearable fifteen minutes of me watching him prepare the instruments for my eventual torture, Pea Daddy finally drained the meat and started preparing the sauce from his mom's Suzy's Zoo recipe card. Some gloppy brown goop came out of a can. Some dehydrated onion powder was sprinkled atop. And then a look of sheer panic washed over Pea Daddy's face.

"I gotta go. I forgot something," he spat frantically.

"Are you going to the store? Do you want me to go with you?" I said sweetly, considering adding, "Can we stop and get something to eat on the way there?"

"No. I'll be right back."

Pea Daddy walked out the front door, no wallet, no keys, no jacket, and I knew I was in trouble. As soon as I heard the last of his footsteps down the stairs outside, I ran to his bedroom window. I pulled up his shade and, horrified, saw Pea Daddy sprinting to the McDonald's across the street. This was going to be good. And by good, I mean completely disgusting.

I went in and sat on the couch and pondered whether or not my parents would be responsible for my law school loans when I was dead from stroganoff.

Pea Daddy returned shortly and quickly said, "You just stay in there and relax. I'll call you when it's ready."

Oh, please don't.

But he did. And as I sat down to a steaming plate of boiled beef, brown glop, onion powder and a mystery ingredient from the Golden Arches, I spied three used packets of "fancy catsup" on the edge of the counter. Dinner was not good. Ketchup does not belong in stroganoff. But at least Pea Daddy had the good sense not to pay for it.

And that's just one more reason he handles the finances. But, dear Lord, please leave the stroganoff to me.

INGREDIENTS

2 tablespoons cornstarch

1 cup water

cooking spray or oil, to grease skillet

1 cup yellow onion, thinly sliced

1 8-ounce package tempeh

2 teaspoons garlic, minced

¾ cup vegetable stock

2 tablespoons balsamic vinegar

1 tablespoon reduced-sodium soy sauce

2 teaspoons vegan Worcestershire sauce

¾ cup nondairy milk (unflavored, unsweetened) or organic milk

1 tablespoon Dijon mustard

⅓ cup nutritional yeast

1 tablespoon Italian seasoning

1 tablespoon dried parsley

1 teaspoon salt

8 ounces whole-grain fusilli (wheat, rice, etc.), cooked according to package directions

DIRECTIONS

1 Mix cornstarch and water together in a small bowl and set aside.

2 Lightly coat a large, deep skillet with cooking spray or oil and place over medium-high heat.

3 Sauté onion until softened but not yet browned, about 3 minutes.

4 Grate tempeh into skillet using a large-holed grater. Sauté with onion until toasty and brown, about 3 to 4 minutes. Add garlic to the skillet and cook for an additional minute.

5 Add vegetable stock, balsamic vinegar, soy sauce, Worcestershire sauce, milk, mustard, nutritional yeast, Italian seasoning, parsley and salt to the skillet and bring to a low boil over high heat.

6 Add cornstarch mixture, whisking rapidly. Lower heat and let sauce thicken, stirring frequently, for about 5 minutes.

7 Place fusilli in individual bowls and top with stroganoff.

NUTRITION INFORMATION PER SERVING: 410 calories, 9 g total fat, 2.5 g saturated fat, 0 g trans fat, 30 mg cholesterol, 910 mg sodium, 58 g carbohydrate, 7 g fiber, 6 g sugar, 29 g protein, vitamin A 4%, vitamin C 4%, calcium 15%, iron 20%

Dinners

Roasted Chickpea Tacos

Makes 8 tacos

more peas, thank you

WE LOVE TACOS.

Messy, crunchy, "take a big bite and spill half of it down your face" tacos. I'd been roasting chickpeas for ages when it finally dawned on me that they didn't just belong in my face. They belonged in a taco shell. Or in my case, in a taco shell, then on my shirt, then in my face.

The tacos first appeared on our website in August 2010 and they've been one of our most popular recipes ever since. The zesty, slightly spicy chickpeas get chewy and crunchy and are totally irresistible. Reader Stephanie says, "The chickpea tacos are one of my favorite recipeas. My eighteen-month-old sous chef eats half of the chickpea mixture out of the bowl she is mixing before they are even cooked!"

Sounds like she needs a new sous chef. I wonder if she'll loan me her bib, though.

INGREDIENTS

2 teaspoons chili powder

¼ teaspoon garlic powder

¼ teaspoon onion powder

¼ teaspoon dried oregano

1½ teaspoons cumin

1 teaspoon sea salt

1 tablespoon lime juice

2 tablespoons water

1 14-ounce can chickpeas, drained and rinsed

cooking spray, to grease baking sheet

8 corn taco shells

shredded lettuce, chopped tomato, Almost Chipotle Guacamole (p. 96), nondairy cheese (i.e., Daiya) or organic cheese, sliced black olives, minced cilantro, to garnish

DIRECTIONS

1 Preheat oven to 375 degrees F.

2 In a large bowl, combine chili powder, garlic powder, onion powder, oregano, cumin, salt, lime juice and water. Add chickpeas and marinate for at least 30 minutes.

3 Place chickpeas on a baking sheet that has been sprayed with cooking spray.

4 Bake for 20 to 30 minutes, stirring once during cooking, or until chickpeas are slightly crispy.

5 Prepare taco shells according to package directions. Fill with chickpeas and desired toppings.

NUTRITION INFORMATION PER SERVING: 120 calories, 1.5 g total fat, 0 g saturated fat, 0 g trans fat, 0 mg cholesterol, 450 mg sodium, 24 g carbohydrate, 4 g fiber, 0 g sugar, 4 g protein, vitamin A 0%, vitamin C 4%, calcium 6%, iron 8%

Toppings not included in analysis.

pea points

Make a double or even a triple batch of the roasted chickpeas and put them on top of salads, stuff them in pitas with all your trimmings, or just eat them by the handful as an after-school snack.

Dinners

Portabella Mushroom Fajitas

Serves 4

PEOPLE LIKE SIZZLE.

I once had a high school teacher write about me on a college recommendation, "If you were to solely judge a steak by its sizzle, you'd be making a mistake when it comes to Sarah." Ouch.

I'd hate to think of what a teacher who didn't like me would say. I'm not denying that I didn't exactly "sizzle" my way through high school. Let's just say discovering tweezers and realizing that they could be used to removed that patch of hair between your eyebrows was a skill I learned late in life. And wax or bleaching cream for upper lips? Forget about it.

Yes, people love the sizzle. Perhaps that's why fajitas are so darn popular at Mexican restaurants. They're the homecoming queen. They enter the room and everyone oohs and aahs. They're loud, hissing and spitting at everyone around them. Everyone shies away in fear that if they are not careful, they might get burned. And finally everyone looks to see who the noisy, delicious dish belongs to.

I wrote off becoming homecoming queen. What my peers had against facial hair, I'll never know. And when we gave up eating meat, I wrote off fajitas too. Until now. Another skill I learned late in life was how to transform portabella mushrooms into something deliciously spectacular all their own. Turns out, if you marinate these meaty 'shrooms in traditional fajita spices and flavorings, something beautiful happens.

There's no noisy, dangerous platter. No hissing or spitting. No attention-grabbing entrance. These are just some darn tasty eats. And if you were to judge these fajitas solely by their sizzle, you'd be making a mistake.

A big, hairy mistake.

173

Dinners

INGREDIENTS

2 teaspoons organic
Worcestershire sauce

2 teaspoons reduced-sodium
soy sauce

2 teaspoons apple cider
vinegar

½ teaspoon liquid smoke
(optional)

1 teaspoon garlic, minced

½ teaspoon chili powder

½ teaspoon cumin

1 large bell pepper, thinly sliced

1 medium yellow onion,
thinly sliced

2 large portabella mushroom
caps, cleaned and sliced into
½-inch strips

cooking spray or oil, to grease
skillet

squeeze of fresh lime juice

8 corn tortillas

shredded nondairy cheese
(i.e., Daiya) or organic cheese,
salsa, shredded lettuce, minced
fresh cilantro, Almost Chipotle
Guacamole (p. 96), to garnish

DIRECTIONS

1   In a large bowl, whisk together Worcestershire sauce, soy sauce,
    vinegar, liquid smoke, garlic, chili powder and cumin.

2   Add the peppers, onions and mushrooms to the marinade and toss
    until evenly distributed. Cover and marinate in the refrigerator for
    at least an hour or overnight.

3   Drain peppers, onions and mushrooms and sauté in a medium skillet
    lightly greased with cooking spray or oil over medium-high heat.
    Cook 5 to 7 minutes, or until peppers and onions are tender and
    mushrooms are lightly seared.

4   Season vegetables with lime juice.

5   Prepare corn tortillas by wrapping them in damp paper towels and
    heating them in a microwave or warm oven. Fill each tortilla with
    the fajita mixture and garnish with any desired toppings.

pea points

Throw leftover
fajitas in with your
tofu scramble and
use the combo to fill
flour tortillas for a
delicious breakfast
burrito. It's sizzlin'.

NUTRITION INFORMATION PER SERVING: 160 calories, 1.5 g total fat, 0 g saturated fat,
0 g trans fat, 0 mg cholesterol, 135 mg sodium, 33 g carbohydrate, 5 g fiber, 3 g sugar,
5 g protein, vitamin A 4%, vitamin C 60%, calcium 10%, iron 6%

Optional ingredients and toppings not included in analysis.

more peas, thank you

Sloppy Josephines

Makes 8 sandwiches with approximately ½ cup filling each

THE GIRLS ARE STILL AT THAT AGE WHERE BOYS ARE "ICKY."

Thank goodness. I'll take it as long as I can. It doesn't always make life easier, though. I've stood in the longest line at Target multiple times, buying one thing I needed and eighteen I didn't, staring at the magazines, counting the gum packs, waiting, waiting, waiting. Just because Lulu wanted to "go to the girl."

Of course, there has been more than one occasion where the gender of our clerk was undetermined and I had to publicly explain in the most private way possible that the lovely young person helping us was in fact a girl. We did not get a free sticker those days.

When it comes to dinner, I don't mess around. Sloppy Joe is not invited. But Sloppy Josephine? *She* is the guest of honor. And she's been honored at many tables of *Peas and Thank You Blog* readers, including Annie, who says, "This is quite possibly one of the very best easy dishes that's ever come out of my kitchen. I adored it! And will adore it again when I eat the leftovers tonight. And tomorrow night."

For the record, Lulu, you can relax. Annie is a girl. And a girl with good taste at that.

INGREDIENTS

4 cups vegetable broth or water

1 cup dried lentils, rinsed and drained

cooking spray or oil, to grease skillet

½ cup yellow onion, chopped

2 cloves garlic, minced

1 tablespoon chili powder

2 teaspoons dried oregano

1 14-ounce can tomato sauce

¼ cup tomato paste

1 tablespoon red wine vinegar

1 tablespoon vegan Worcestershire sauce

¼ cup all-natural barbecue sauce

salt and pepper to taste

8 whole wheat hamburger buns, split and toasted

4 pickles, sliced

INGREDIENTS

1 Bring broth or water to boil in a medium pot over medium-high heat. Add lentils, bring to a boil, lower heat and cook until tender, approximately 30 minutes.

2 Drain lentils and set aside.

3 To a skillet that has been lightly greased with cooking spray or oil, add onions and sauté over medium heat until onions start to soften and brown, about 5 minutes.

4 Add garlic, chili powder and oregano and sauté for 1 to 2 minutes.

5 Add tomato sauce, tomato paste, red wine vinegar, Worcestershire sauce and barbecue sauce. Stir to combine and then add lentils. Mix thoroughly and season with salt and pepper to taste.

6 Scoop lentil mixture onto toasted buns and garnish with pickles.

NUTRITION INFORMATION PER SERVING: 270 calories, 3 g total fat, 0.5 saturated fat, 0 g trans fat, 0 mg cholesterol, 910 mg sodium, 50 g carbohydrate, 11 g fiber, 14 g sugar, 12 g protein, vitamin A 15%, vitamin C 10%, calcium 6%, iron 25%

Chickpeas and Dumplings

Makes 4 servings

THEY SAID IT COULDN'T BE DONE.

Make comfort food from plants? A craveable dish hearty enough to satisfy husbands, boyfriends and teenagers? A meal that's low in fat and high in flavor? A dinner that costs less than $1.29 per serving? That's also gluten free? Had I not come up with this dish for Sunday supper one night, and for dozens and dozens of Sunday suppers since, I wouldn't have believed it myself.

But tasting is believing. And lots of *Peas and Thank You* readers believe. Like Jessica, who says, "I made this for dinner and my every-kind-of-meat-loving hubby took one bite, looked at me and said, 'I hate you.' Of course, I said, 'Cool. Thanks. Why?' and he said, 'Because you make meatless meals so insanely delicious that I don't even miss the meat.'"

And they said it couldn't be done.

INGREDIENTS

Chickpea stew base: cooking spray or oil, to grease pot

1 cup yellow onion, chopped

1 cup celery, chopped

1 medium carrot, peeled and chopped

1 tablespoon garlic, minced

½ teaspoon salt

¾ teaspoon curry powder

½ teaspoon dried oregano

¾ teaspoon dried rosemary

½ teaspoon dried basil

4 cups vegetable stock

1 14-ounce can chickpeas, drained and rinsed

1 tablespoon apple cider vinegar

2 tablespoons cornstarch

Dumplings:
½ cup gluten-free all-purpose flour

½ cup gluten-free oat flour (see pea points on p. 179)

1 teaspoon baking powder

½ teaspoon baking soda

½ teaspoon salt

½ teaspoon dried oregano

½ teaspoon dried basil

½ cup nondairy milk or organic milk

1 tablespoon vegan margarine (i.e., Earth Balance) or organic butter, melted

DIRECTIONS

1   Grease a large pot with cooking spray or oil and place over medium-high heat. Add onion, celery and carrot and sauté for 4 to 5 minutes, or until vegetables have slightly softened and started to brown. Add garlic, salt, curry, oregano, rosemary and basil and sauté for an additional minute, or until aromatic.

2   Carefully pour in vegetable stock, chickpeas and vinegar and bring to a low boil.

3   Put the cornstarch in a small bowl and add a ladleful of the hot broth from the pot. Whisk to remove any lumps.

4   Pour the cornstarch mixture into the pot, stirring vigorously. Return to a boil and then reduce heat to low and cover.

5   To prepare the dumplings, in a medium bowl combine flours, baking powder, baking soda, salt, oregano and basil. Add milk and melted margarine or butter, and stir until a dough just forms. Do not overmix.

6   Drop dough by the heaping tablespoonful on top of stew. Cover and simmer on low heat for 15 to 17 minutes, or until dumplings are cooked through.

7   As much as you may want to lift the lid to peek at the dumplings, don't do it.

8   Serve while hot and slightly doughy.

NUTRITION INFORMATION PER SERVING: 340 calories, 5 g total fat, 1.5 g saturated fat, 0 g trans fat, 0 mg cholesterol, 1740 mg sodium, 66 g carbohydrate, 8 g fiber, 9 g sugar, 10 g protein, vitamin A 110%, vitamin C 15%, calcium 10%, iron 15%

pea points

You can make your own gluten-free oat flour by grinding gluten-free oats in a blender or food processor. If gluten is not a concern for you, make these dumplings with ½ cup each of unbleached all-purpose flour and whole wheat pastry flour.

Dinners

Black-Eyed Pea Veggie Burgers

Makes 4 patties

THERE IS A SERIOUS CRIME BEING PERPETRATED AGAINST NON-
MEAT EATERS IN RESTAURANTS ACROSS THE NATION—THE FROZEN
VEGGIE BURGER.

Not much irks me more than ordering up a burger and paying twice as
much in a restaurant for something I have sitting in my freezer at home.
But if I walk into a restaurant and see a house-made veggie burger on
the menu, I'm all over it. Well, really I just make Pea Daddy order it so
I can have a big bite. And half his fries. It's in our marriage vows.

The tricky thing about veggie burgers—and the reason why so many
of us at home and in restaurants reach for that box in the freezer—is that
they aren't easy to do well. They fall apart. They're too beany. They're
too mushy. Or they are just plain bland. In my quest for the perfect
veggie burger, I've come up with what might very well be the solution.
They hold up well in the pan. They have an amazing texture, with the right
little cornmeal crunch. And they are perfectly spiced with lime, cumin
and chili powder.

Save room in the freezer for ice cream and save room in your belly
for these burgers.

INGREDIENTS

1 14-ounce can black-eyed peas,
drained and rinsed

1 large white potato, peeled,
cubed, steamed and mashed

1 tablespoon extra-virgin olive oil

½ cup yellow onion, chopped

½ cup corn (fresh or frozen,
then defrosted)

1 teaspoon garlic, minced

1 tablespoon lime juice

1 tablespoon cumin

1½ teaspoons chili powder

2 tablespoons fresh cilantro,
minced

¼ cup cornmeal

salt and pepper to taste

cooking spray or olive oil,
to grease skillet

4 whole wheat hamburger buns,
split and toasted

DIRECTIONS

1 Using a fork or a potato masher, mash the black-eyed peas and potato together until smooth, yet slightly chunky. Add oil, onion, corn, garlic, lime juice, cumin, chili powder, cilantro, cornmeal and salt and pepper to taste and mix well.

2 Chill mixture for at least 30 minutes in the refrigerator.

3 Using your hands, form mixture into patties.

4 Place a large skillet greased with cooking spray or olive oil over medium-high heat. Add burgers to the skillet and cook for 5 to 6 minutes on each side.

5 Serve veggie burgers on toasted buns and top with the trimmings of your choice.

NUTRITION INFORMATION PER SERVING: 240 calories, 4.5 g total fat, 0.5 saturated fat, 0 g trans fat, 0 mg cholesterol, 320 mg sodium, 44 g carbohydrate, 7 g fiber, 2 g sugar, 9 g protein, vitamin A 8%, vitamin C 45%, calcium 6%, iron 15%

Black Bean Dal

Makes 4 servings of approximately 1½ cups each

I'VE GOT SOME MAGIC BEANS TO SELL YOU.

They've made their way into so many of my recipes, I've lost count. Veggie burgers, soups, casseroles and even a batch of brownies that quite intentionally didn't make the cut for this book. You're welcome.

Black beans make Lulu smile as she eats them straight from the can. That's hard-core. They make an otherwise tone-deaf family decidedly musical. That's gross. Sorry. They make Pea Daddy eat Indian food. That's nothing short of a miracle. A few negative experiences at some sketchy buffets had turned him off to an entire country's cuisine. Until now. All it took was my magic beans.

INGREDIENTS

cooking spray or oil, to grease skillet

½ cup yellow onion, chopped

1 tablespoon fresh ginger, minced

1½ teaspoons garlic, minced

1 teaspoon cumin

1 teaspoon turmeric

1 14-ounce can organic fire-roasted tomatoes (i.e., Muir Glen)

1 14-ounce can black beans, drained and rinsed

1 lime, juiced

1 tablespoon fresh cilantro, minced

salt and pepper to taste

DIRECTIONS

1   Place a large skillet greased lightly with cooking spray or oil over medium-high heat. Add onion and sauté for 5 to 6 minutes, or until softened. Add ginger, garlic, cumin and turmeric and sauté for an additional minute, or until aromatic.

2   Add tomatoes and black beans and bring to a low simmer. Reduce heat and cook for 10 to 12 minutes.

3   Stir in lime juice and cilantro. Season with salt and pepper to taste. Serve dal over cooked brown rice, millet, quinoa or any grain of choice.

NUTRITION INFORMATION PER SERVING: 130 calories, 0.5 g total fat, 0 g saturated fat, 0 g trans fat, 0 mg cholesterol, 610 mg sodium, 25 g carbohydrate, 8 g fiber, 4 g sugar, 7 g protein, vitamin A 8%, vitamin C 40%, calcium 8%, iron 20%

Dinners

Desserts

Coconut Cream
Doughnuts 186

Thin Mint Cookies 189

Pumpkin Gingersnap
Cookie Dough Balls 191

Fluffernut Brownies 194

Old-Fashioned
Pumpkin Pie 198

Snickerdoodle Cookie
Dough Balls 201

Orange Chocolate
Dream Pie 204

Oatmeal Chocolate
Chip Cookies 207

Apple Cider
Doughnuts 210

S'mores Bread
Pudding 213

Apple Crisp 215

Gingerbread Cupcakes
with Lemon Cheesecake
Frosting 218

Root Beer
Cupcakes 221

Peach Cobbler 224

Better Cake Pops 226

Blueberry
Doughnuts 229

Banana Pudding
with Vanilla Wafers 232

Chocolate Peppermint
Brownie Cake Pops 235

Coconut Cream Doughnuts

Makes 1 dozen doughnuts

IF YOU AREN'T A PARENT, CHANCES ARE YOU WILL THINK I AM A HORRIBLE PERSON AFTER READING THIS.

The thing is, if you aren't a parent, you really haven't ever had to share everything. Sure, you may have twelve siblings and thirty-eight cousins, but you still haven't *really* had to share everything. Chapstick. Gum. Ice cubes. Toilet paper.

This explains why I use only very bright lipstick, which no child can touch. The mailman thinks I have the hots for him, as I head down to the mailbox in the morning with a fiery red kisser. Of course, the crazy hairdo and the mismatched socks might just make him think I'm, well, crazy.

I buy only Atomic cinnamon gum. Just the smell makes 'em cry. They don't dare ask for a piece. Not even Pea Daddy. I make my ice cubes out of pure vodka. Okay, no, I don't, but that's a really good idea. And as for toilet paper, we are a two-ply family all the way. One ply for you, one ply for me.

That's not to say that the whole "Mommy, I want some of that, can I have some of that, gimme some of that!" scenario hasn't worked in my favor. Gigi's favorite food is spinach. 'Nuff said. But that doesn't mean that I don't go out of my way to make things that my girls will never, ever beg for. Things like Coconut Cream Doughnuts.

I don't know when my girls got it into their heads that they don't like coconut. But that day is among the happiest of my life, right up there with my wedding day, the day of their births and the day a shirtless Ryan Reynolds on the cover of *Entertainment Weekly* appeared in my mailbox. I really did kiss the mailman that day.

While I have plenty of doughnut recipes and toppings that the girls do love, when I want something just for me, I put on my lipstick, grab an ice-cold glass of "water" and serve myself one of these doughnuts.

With extra coconut.

INGREDIENTS

1½ cups unbleached all-purpose flour

¾ cup whole wheat pastry flour

1 tablespoon baking powder

¼ teaspoon salt

¼ teaspoon nutmeg

¼ cup vegan margarine (i.e., Earth Balance), melted

1¼ cups reduced-fat or regular coconut milk

½ teaspoon coconut extract

1 cup organic sugar

cooking spray, to grease pan

Topping:
1 cup organic powdered sugar

3 tablespoons coconut butter

3 tablespoons reduced-fat or regular coconut milk

¼ teaspoon coconut extract

pinch of salt

1 cup unsweetened coconut, toasted

DIRECTIONS

1   Preheat oven to 350 degrees F.

2   In a medium bowl, combine flours, baking powder, salt and nutmeg.

3   In a small bowl combine melted margarine, coconut milk, coconut extract and sugar. Mix until sugar has dissolved.

4   Add milk mixture to flour mixture and stir until just combined.

5   Pipe or spoon batter into a doughnut pan that has been lightly greased with cooking spray.

6   Bake for 11 to 13 minutes, or until doughnuts are firm to the touch. Allow doughnuts to cool in the pan for approximately 5 minutes before transferring to a cooling rack.

7   To prepare the topping, beat together powdered sugar, coconut butter, coconut milk, coconut extract and salt.

8   Frost each doughnut and top with toasted coconut.

pea points

To toast the coconut, place it in a dry skillet over medium-low heat and stir frequently until golden brown. In the alternative, place the coconut in a microwave-safe dish and heat in forty-five-second intervals, stirring after each, until golden brown.

NUTRITION INFORMATION PER SERVING: 180 calories, 8 g total fat, 4.5 g saturated fat, 0 g trans fat, 0 mg cholesterol, 170 mg sodium, 27 g carbohydrate, 2 g fiber, 9 g sugar, 3 g protein, vitamin A 0%, vitamin C 0%, calcium 0%, iron 4%

Based on 12 doughnuts.

more peas, thank you

Thin Mint Cookies

Makes 15 to 20 cookies

This recipe was inspired by the Girl Scout Thin Mint Cookies that magically appear at my doorstep once a year.

I WAS NEVER A GIRL SCOUT.

I always wanted to be one, but probably not for the right reasons. First, there were the adorable uniforms, the crisp white shirts, wool skirts and knee socks, garb not at all appropriate for the tree climbing, fort building and big brother wrestling I was used to. Then there was the actual name of the troop I wanted to be a part of: Brownies. It still makes my mouth water. Finally, there was the most important reason of all—those tasty little cookies.

My mom always bought a box or two whenever those enviable little scouts came to our door, and she always hid the box of her favorite kind in the back of the freezer for safekeeping. Unfortunately for her, it didn't really preserve her cookies from our grubby clutches. It just taught us to enjoy our cookies frozen. Oh, do I ever.

I don't buy the cookies myself anymore, but I do make my own. And I bet you know exactly where I like to keep them. Just don't tell my kids.

Desserts

INGREDIENTS

½ cup whole wheat pastry flour

½ cup unbleached all-purpose flour

½ cup organic sugar

½ cup cocoa powder

½ teaspoon baking powder

½ teaspoon baking soda

½ teaspoon salt

½ cup unsweetened applesauce

¼ cup plus 1 teaspoon coconut oil

¼ cup nondairy milk or organic milk

2 teaspoons vanilla extract

½ cup nondairy chocolate chips

2 teaspoons mint extract

DIRECTIONS

1 Preheat oven to 375 degrees F.

2 In a large bowl, combine flours, sugar, cocoa powder, baking powder, baking soda and salt.

3 In a small bowl, mix together applesauce, ¼ cup of the coconut oil, milk and vanilla.

4 Add wet ingredients to flour mixture and blend until just combined.

5 Scoop dough out with a small scoop or a tablespoon and place an inch or two apart on an ungreased cookie sheet. Press each into a circle with your fingers.

6 Bake cookies for 12 to 14 minutes. Allow cookies to cool completely on the cookie sheet.

7 To prepare chocolate coating, melt together chocolate chips, the remaining teaspoon of coconut oil and mint extract in the microwave or a double boiler. Dip the top of each cookie into the mint chocolate mixture and transfer to a wax paper–lined plate or platter. Refrigerate for at least 20 minutes, or until chocolate is set, before eating.

NUTRITION INFORMATION PER SERVING: 80 calories, 4 g total fat, 3 g saturated fat, 0 g trans fat, 0 mg cholesterol, 100 mg sodium, 9 g carbohydrate, 0 g fiber, 5 g sugar, <1 g protein, vitamin A 0%, vitamin C 0%, calcium 0%, iron 2%

Based on 20 cookies.

Pumpkin Gingersnap Cookie Dough Balls

Makes 20 to 24 cookies

IT SEEMS FUNNY TO SIT DOWN AND WRITE A STORY ABOUT MY GRANDPA'S FAVORITE COOKIE WHEN REALLY IT'S JUST STARTING TO DAWN ON ME JUST HOW MUCH I DIDN'T KNOW ABOUT THE MAN.

He married my grandmother on my mother's twenty-first birthday. In Vegas. My grandparents! It wasn't the first marriage for either one, so I guess that makes him my step-grandpa. To me he was always just Papa Bud.

I don't know anything about Papa Bud's life before he married my grandma. He had a few tattoos, which I thought might have some sort of military basis, but Mom told me not to ask. He had a picture of his daughter and granddaughter tacked up on the refrigerator, between a Maxine cartoon and a magnet with a kitten falling off a tree branch that said "Hang in there!" I always wondered about this little girl, his other granddaughter, but never asked about her. I wondered what they got her for Christmas and if it was her favorite pair of slippers wrapped in an old pipe tobacco can. My Papa Bud liked pipes, and I loved the smell of the tobacco, which explains why I was always sniffing my slippers.

He was a big man, with a scratchy gray beard and twinkling eyes. He easily could have passed for Santa, and if the beard didn't sell it, his robust laugh certainly would. That and the suspenders. Jolly doesn't even begin to describe him. He'd sit in his big leather recliner and we'd cuddle up on his lap. He'd start tickling me, and I would scream with delight, finally calling out to my brother to come rescue me. "Eddie...help! Help...Eddie!" And he'd reply in a silly way, saying, "Eddie doesn't need any help!" and tickle me some more. I loved it.

Desserts

Papa Bud worked as a security guard in the mall and I loved going to visit him when we had shopping to do. I'm not sure if he had a gun or not, but he might as well have for all the importance his dark blue uniform, handcuffs and badge possessed for me. But authority meant nothing next to the lure of the food court, and visiting Papa Bud meant I got one of those frosted chocolate cookies the size of my head with the gooey marshmallow center. To this day I think those might be the best cookies in the whole wide world—which is exactly why this story about Papa Bud's favorite cookie makes so little sense to me.

If you had access to hot, gooey chocolate pillows of heaven with a fluffy cloud of marshmallow crème in the center every single day of your life on the job, why on God's green earth would a molasses ginger-snap be your favorite cookie? Why would you shoo off Christmas gifts like bird feeders and back scratchers and simply ask for a giant jar of homemade gingersnaps?

I never did find out all I wish I knew about Papa Bud. But that doesn't mean I didn't love him. Or that when I make gingersnaps during the holi-days each year, I don't think of him and wonder if that little girl on the refrigerator misses him as much as I do.

INGREDIENTS

2 cups whole wheat pastry flour

1 tablespoon ground ginger

2 teaspoons baking soda

½ teaspoon baking powder

1 teaspoon cinnamon

½ cup vegan margarine (i.e., Earth Balance)

½ cup canned pumpkin

1 cup organic sugar plus ¼ cup for rolling

¼ cup molasses

DIRECTIONS

1   In a medium bowl, combine flour, ginger, baking soda, baking powder and cinnamon. Set aside.

2   Using an electric handheld mixer or a stand mixer, beat together margarine, pumpkin, the cup of sugar and molasses. Gradually add flour mixture to pumpkin mixture, mixing until a dough comes together. Chill dough for at least an hour.

3   When dough is chilled, preheat oven to 350 degrees F and pour remaining ¼ cup of sugar into a shallow bowl. Roll heaping tablespoons of dough into balls. Roll each ball in the sugar until completely covered. Place balls an inch apart on an ungreased cookie sheet. Using the base of a drinking glass or the palm of your hand, flatten the balls.

4   Bake cookies for 8 to 10 minutes, or until the edges have set. Do not overbake. Cookies will seem soft, but allow them to cool on the cookie sheet for 1 to 2 minutes before transferring them to a cooling rack.

NUTRITION INFORMATION PER SERVING: 120 calories, 4 g total fat, 1 g saturated fat, 0 g trans fat, 0 mg cholesterol, 120 mg sodium, 20 g carbohydrate, 2 g fiber, 12 g sugar, 1 g protein, vitamin A 15%, vitamin C 0%, calcium 0%, iron 2%

Based on 24 cookies.

Fluffernut Brownies

Makes 12 brownies

I WAS A NICE LITTLE GIRL.

I looked a lot like Gigi, but without the crazy hair and overflowing spunk. I wasn't into dancing and singing; I was into reading and reading. In other words, the teachers loved me and the other kids didn't. So when I was in fourth grade and met the new girl, Maegan, I saw it as my chance to make a new friend that didn't live on a shelf in the library, give me paper cuts or strain my already grossly nearsighted eyes.

Maegan had everything I didn't, including blond hair, braces, acting lessons, lip gloss, pageant trophies and self-confidence. We became friends right away, mostly because she hadn't met anyone else yet and she lived a block away. I loved going to her house, where she lived with her stepdad, mom and little sister, because there I could try on the braces that her Cabbage Patch Kid wore, don a pageant sash and lip gloss and pretend to be anyone but me. I secretly started wishing that my parents would get divorced so I could have a stepfamily with at least one sister instead of my brothers, and I started adding an extra vowel to my name. "It's spelled S-a-r-a-e-h."

As if that weren't enough, Maegan's family had a pool. Before you act unimpressed, you must realize we live in Oregon. Having a pool is about as necessary as me getting a bikini wax: the upkeep is hardly worth the slight chance that there will be any payoff. Of course, it wasn't just a Mr. Turtle. This was a full-size inground swimming pool with a diving board, and to my horror now, a makeshift high dive that was actually a two-by-four placed on the railing of the upper patio deck. (Note to self: never allow Gigi or Lulu to make friends with kids who have pools.)

It was on one of those rare days that we were actually able to use the pool that a batch of brownies corrupted me. We were sitting by the pool, me in my faded black one-piece and Maegan in her bright rainbow-colored suit with heart cutouts down the sides. Maegan's little sister Molly was a few feet away, swinging on the family's huge play structure.

I'm sure guilt has tainted my memory, but Molly was as sweet as they come, with her long brown braids tied off with silky blue ribbons, her freckled nose and her big brown eyes. She was happy to let Maegan be the "star" of the family, and Maegan always made sure she knew her place when I was over, which was slightly beneath me and far beneath Maegan in the "hierarchy of awesomeness." Perhaps this should have served as a forewarning to Molly, who came running like an oblivious golden retriever when Maegan called her over to us.

We'd been eating some brownies that Maegan's mom had made from a box, which in my "from-scratch baking only" house was a sign of a life of luxury. As if the blissful Betty Crocker treats weren't enough, we were eating the brownies with the little Dixie cups of vanilla ice cream that came with tiny wooden spoons. Now that was just plain frivolous. Perhaps it was a toxic combination of Aqua Net and Bonne Bell, but Maegan suddenly had the diabolical idea to trick Molly into eating dirt.

"Molly, do you want a brownie sundae?" Maegan called over to her intended victim. I watched with horror as Maegan scooped up a handful of dirt from her mother's flower bed, dropped it into her Dixie cup and gave it a vigorous stir. I don't know if it was not wanting to cross this friend that I idolized or just being on the receiving end of enough abuse from my own brothers, but I did nothing to stop her and, in fact, helped with the hard sell.

I grabbed a clump of brownie and stirred it into my own ice cream. As I lifted a bite up to my unglossed lips, I remember my own private secondhand acting lessons that Maegan had given me and convincingly said, "Mmmm…you've got to try this!"

Molly skipped over to the pool, her braids bouncing in the sunlight and her eyes filled with a glimmer of hope that she might fall into her big sister's favor. "Okay!"

I was instantly filled with regret as she took a big scoop and put the Triple Potting Soil Swirl in her mouth. It took only a moment for her to realize what she was eating. As Molly spit the ice cream out and burst into tears, I saw it as my time to go. I grabbed my terry-cloth green cover-up and my dirty lace-free Keds and ran home like there was going to be a New Kids on the Block concert on our front lawn.

Maegan and I grew apart as we got older. She got a car and a boyfriend, and I got a bad perm and a journal with a cat playing with a ball of yarn on the cover. Not long ago, I ran into Molly at a park, where she was chasing her four freckled little boys around. She told me about Maegan's amazing life now, that she does missionary work in Costa Rica and has a husband and three little girls of her own. As we parted ways, we made the promise that all moms make regardless of whether they intend to follow through or not. "Let's make a playdate!"

I just know if that playdate ever comes to fruition, I will not be serving brownies, though I've got a recipe. And there are only good things mixed in.

INGREDIENTS

¾ cup whole wheat pastry flour

¾ cup unbleached
all-purpose flour

⅔ cup cocoa powder

1 tablespoon baking powder

1 teaspoon baking soda

1 teaspoon salt

1½ cups unsweetened
applesauce

1 cup natural peanut butter

⅔ cup organic sugar

1 teaspoon vanilla extract

cooking spray, to grease pan

½ cup vegan marshmallow
crème (i.e., Suzanne's
Ricemellow Creme)

DIRECTIONS

1   Preheat oven to 350 degrees F.

2   In a large bowl, combine flours, cocoa powder, baking powder,
    baking soda and salt.

3   In a medium bowl, combine applesauce, ½ cup of the peanut butter,
    sugar and vanilla.

4   Add applesauce mixture to dry ingredients and stir until just
    combined. Pour batter into an 8 x 8-inch pan that's been greased
    with cooking spray.

5   Spoon remaining ½ cup peanut butter and, separately, marsh-
    mallow crème by the tablespoonful on top of the brownie batter.
    Using a knife, make lines horizontally across the batter and then
    vertically to create a swirl pattern in the peanut butter and
    marshmallow crème.

6   Bake for 30 to 35 minutes, or until the brownies have set and
    the edges have started to pull away from the pan. Let cool
    before cutting.

NUTRITION INFORMATION PER SERVING: 290 calories, 12 g total fat, 2.5 g saturated fat,
0 g trans fat, 0 mg cholesterol, 220 mg sodium, 39 g carbohydrate, 4 g fiber, 21 g sugar,
8 g protein, vitamin A 0%, vitamin C 4%, calcium 0%, iron 10%

Old-Fashioned Pumpkin Pie

Makes one 9-inch pie

This recipe was inspired by the pumpkin pie we all have enjoyed every Thanksgiving. Go call the person who made it for you and give thanks.

I LOVE THE ENGLISH LANGUAGE, BUT A FEW PHRASES REALLY GET UNDER MY SKIN.

"I'm sorry you feel that way." Biggest cop-out ever, except for the even more insulting, "I'm sorry *if* you really feel that way." Now you're not sorry, and I'm a liar. Awesome. "It is what it is." Thanks, Yoda. "Whoever smelt it, dealt it." I'm not sure anything could be less true. Except this one, which is a little more relevant to the topic at hand. "Easy as pie!" You know who says "Easy as pie!"? The person who buys frozen pie.

I'm not sure there are many tasks *less* easy than making a pie, but ever since my grandmother passed away, before Gigi was born, I've been the pie maker in my family. I'm getting better, trying to implement as many of Grandma's techniques as I can. Not overhandling the dough. Baking the pie a day in advance. Always keeping a box of wine tapped in the pantry. Okay, maybe not that last one.

more peas, thank you

Nevertheless, Grandma never stressed if her crust tore a bit when she put it in her pie plate. She never sweated if her edges were not perfectly crimped. And she made it look, well, easy. Maybe she was onto something.

INGREDIENTS

Crust:
1½ cups whole wheat pastry flour

1 teaspoon baking powder

½ teaspoon salt

¼ cup vegan margarine (i.e., Earth Balance) or coconut oil

¼ cup maple syrup

1 teaspoon vanilla extract

2 to 4 tablespoons cold water

Filling:
1 cup nondairy milk or organic milk

½ cup light brown sugar

3 tablespoons cornstarch

2 cups canned pumpkin

1 tablespoon ground flaxseed

1 teaspoon molasses

1 teaspoon vanilla extract

2 teaspoons cinnamon

½ teaspoon salt

½ teaspoon ground ginger

½ teaspoon nutmeg

nondairy or organic whipped topping and pumpkin pie spice, to garnish (optional)

DIRECTIONS

1   To prepare crust, in a large bowl combine flour, baking powder and salt. Cut in margarine or coconut oil until flour mixture has the texture of wet sand. You can also accelerate this process by using a food processor to blend the flour mixture and shortening together. Grandma didn't. I do.

2   In a small liquid measuring cup, combine maple syrup, vanilla and 2 tablespoons of the water. Pour into flour mixture. Stir until a dough starts to form. If the dough seems too dry, add the remaining 1 to 2 tablespoons of water.

3   Transfer dough to a sheet of plastic wrap and wrap it up, pressing it into a disk. Put dough into the refrigerator to chill for at least an hour.

4   Meanwhile, make the filling by bringing ¾ cup of the milk and brown sugar to a boil in a medium saucepan over medium-high heat. Once it has come to a boil, lower heat and simmer.

5   Put cornstarch in a small bowl or a small liquid measuring cup. Add the remaining ¼ cup of milk and stir until completely smooth.

6   Add cornstarch mixture to the saucepan, stirring rapidly. Bring the mixture back to a low boil and cook, stirring frequently, until it is quite thick. Remove from heat.

7   In a large bowl, combine pumpkin, ground flaxseed, molasses, vanilla, cinnamon, salt, ginger and nutmeg. Add sweetened condensed milk and stir until completely incorporated. Set aside.

8   When dough has chilled, preheat oven to 350 degrees F.

9   Dust a breadboard with flour and turn dough out onto it. Roll dough out gently with a floured rolling pin until it is about ¼ inch thick and about 12 inches in diameter.

10 Transfer dough to a 9-inch pie plate by rolling up the edge of the dough on the rolling pin and then unrolling it on top of the pie plate. Or you can invert the breadboard on top of the pie plate. Either way, pray.

11 Press dough into the pie plate and crimp the edges of the crust. Using the tines of a fork, poke holes in the bottom of the pie crust.

12 Pour prepared pumpkin filling into the pie shell and spread evenly.

13 Bake for 45 to 50 minutes, or until pie has set. If you have a pie shield, you'll want to place it over the crust after the pie has baked for about 20 minutes. If you don't have a pie shield, you can make one out of tinfoil, to keep your crust from getting too dark.

14 When the pie is cool, cover and refrigerate, preferably overnight.

200

NUTRITION INFORMATION PER SERVING: 270 calories, 7 g total fat, 2 g saturated fat, 0 g trans fat, 0 mg cholesterol, 400 mg sodium, 48 g carbohydrate, 6 g fiber, 23 g sugar, 5 g protein, vitamin A 150%, vitamin C 2%, calcium 8%, iron 6%

Based on 8 slices of pie. Optional ingredients and toppings not included in analysis.

Snickerdoodle Cookie Dough Balls

Makes 20 to 24 cookies

I DON'T PLAY FAVORITES.

It's just interesting how differently you do things with your second-born versus your first.

If Baby Gigi dropped her Binky on the ground, I had an eight-step sterilization process I went through before giving it back to her. If Lulu dropped her Binky, I wiped it on my pants, stuck it in my own mouth and then gave it back to her.

If anyone wanted to hold Baby Gigi, they had to wash their hands, sit in a completely stable, firm chair and submit to a criminal background check. Mom, I still have questions about that parking ticket from 1988. If anyone wanted to hold Lulu, my response was, "Here, take her! Do I have time for a shower?"

If Baby Gigi took a liking to snickerdoodles around her first birthday, I made multiple batches, running trial after trial, culling recipes from both sides of our family, trying to find the best possible version for her first birthday party. These cookies weren't in place of a birthday cake. They were *in addition* to a birthday cake, handmade and frosted to look exactly like Pea Kitty, minus the scowl. That was a late night. When Lulu wants snickerdoodles, I make these.

When I said I don't play favorites? I lied. These are my favorite.

INGREDIENTS

¾ cup vegan margarine (i.e., Earth Balance)

¾ cup powdered sugar

¼ cup organic sugar plus 2 tablespoons for rolling

½ teaspoon salt

1½ teaspoons vanilla extract

1 cup unbleached all-purpose flour

½ cup whole wheat pastry flour

1½ teaspoons baking powder

up to 1 tablespoon nondairy milk or organic milk

2 teaspoons cinnamon

DIRECTIONS

1 Preheat oven to 350 degrees F.

2 In a stand mixer or using an electric handheld mixer, blend together margarine, powdered sugar, ¼ cup of the organic sugar, salt, vanilla, flours and baking powder.

3 The mixture will look dry, but keep blending until a dough comes together, though it will be crumbly. If the dough cannot be shaped into balls, add milk, being careful to use as little as necessary.

4 In a small bowl, combine the remaining 2 tablespoons of organic sugar and cinnamon.

5 Using a mini scoop or your hands, form dough into golf ball–size balls. Roll dough balls in the cinnamon sugar and place an inch apart on an ungreased baking sheet.

6 Bake for 8 to 10 minutes. The cookies will be delicate when removed from the oven, so allow them to cool for at least 3 minutes before transferring them to a cooling rack.

NUTRITION INFORMATION PER SERVING: 110 calories, 6 g total fat, 1.5 g saturated fat, 0 g trans fat, 0 mg cholesterol, 115 mg sodium, 13 g carbohydrate, 0 g fiber, 7 g sugar, <1 g protein, vitamin A 0%, vitamin C 0%, calcium 0%, iron 2%

Based on 24 cookies.

Desserts

Orange Chocolate Dream Pie

Makes one 9-inch pie

WHENEVER MY MOM AND I RUN INTO ANYONE THAT READS OUR
BLOG OR HAS OUR FIRST BOOK, SHE ALWAYS FEELS A NEED TO
INTRODUCE HERSELF AS "THE ONE WHO COOKS WITH BUTTER
AND BACON."

It's her new name. "Hi. I'm Sarah," I say. "And this is my mom—"

"The One Who Cooks with Butter and Bacon," she interjects.

True, she did cook with butter and bacon. Still does. But she also
started lots of healthy, wonderful food traditions—traditions that I like
to replicate with my girls. She always made homemade bread to pack in
our lunches. (I'll stay mum about the bologna, margarine and mayonnaise
sandwiches.) She never bought cookies in a package but always had
a homemade batch in the oven or in the jar.

And, one of my favorite traditions, she'd always cut up little chunks
of fruit and let us eat them with fondue forks. For a real treat, she'd melt
some chocolate and we'd dip and stab to our heart's content. Mostly
each other, but some fruit too. This recipe was inspired by my favorite
combination, orange segments dipped in chocolate. Often we'd use the
huge leftover oranges that Santa would stick in our stocking.

Because, you know, butter and bacon would just be too messy.

INGREDIENTS

Crust:

1½ cups whole wheat pastry flour

1 teaspoon baking powder

½ teaspoon salt

¼ cup vegan margarine (i.e.,
Earth Balance) or coconut oil

¼ cup maple syrup

1 teaspoon vanilla extract

2 to 4 tablespoons cold water

Filling:

1⅔ cups dark chocolate chips

1 12-ounce package silken tofu,
drained

1 8-ounce tub nondairy cream
cheese (i.e., Tofutti) or organic
cream cheese

2 teaspoons orange extract

candied orange peel, nondairy
or organic whipped cream, fresh
mint, to garnish (optional)

DIRECTIONS

pea points

You can substitute different extracts to create different flavors of pie. Raspberry, almond and even peppermint chocolate pies are equally phenomenal!

1   To prepare crust, in a large bowl, combine flour, baking powder and salt. Cut in margarine or coconut oil until flour mixture has the texture of wet sand.

2   In a small liquid measuring cup, combine maple syrup, vanilla and 2 tablespoons of the water. Pour maple syrup mixture into flour.

3   Stir until a dough starts to form. If the dough seems too dry, add the remaining 1 to 2 tablespoons of water.

4   Transfer dough to a sheet of plastic wrap and wrap it up, pressing it into a disk. Put dough into the refrigerator to chill for at least an hour.

5   When dough has chilled, preheat oven to 350 degrees F.

6   Dust a breadboard with flour and turn dough out onto it. Roll dough out gently with a floured rolling pin until it is about ¼ inch thick and about 12 inches in diameter.

7   Transfer dough to a 9-inch pie plate by rolling up the edge of the dough on the rolling pin and then unrolling it on top of the pie plate. Or you can invert the breadboard on top of the pie plate.

8   Press dough into the pie plate and crimp the edges of the pie crust.

9   Using the tines of a fork, poke holes in the bottom of the pie crust. Line the crust with parchment paper and fill with dried beans or pie weights.

10 Bake pie crust for 20 to 22 minutes, remove parchment and beans or weights and bake for an additional 3 to 5 minutes, or until crust is golden and has set. Allow crust to cool completely.

11 To make filling, melt chocolate chips in a double boiler or in the microwave. Combine chocolate, tofu, cream cheese and orange extract in a food processor or blender and blend until completely smooth.

12 Chill filling in the refrigerator for approximately 30 minutes. Spread filling in cooled crust and chill pie for at least 2 hours or longer before serving. Garnish as desired.

NUTRITION INFORMATION PER SERVING: 280 calories, 13 g total fat, 5 g saturated fat, 0 g trans fat, 0 mg cholesterol, 240 mg sodium, 38 g carbohydrate, 3 g fiber, 18 g sugar, 4 g protein, vitamin A 0%, vitamin C 0%, calcium 2%, iron 2%

Based on 8 slices of pie. Optional ingredients and toppings not included in analysis.

more peas, thank you

Oatmeal Chocolate Chip Cookies

Makes 12 to 15 cookies

I DON'T REALLY HAVE ANYTHING AGAINST RAISINS.

They serve their purpose. Their purpose for me, growing up, was a form of bribery to keep me "regular." It didn't work.

My mom would pour a heaping bowl of Raisin Bran, dump milk over the top and sit it in front of me at the kitchen table. It was a battle of wills. I'd eat all the raisins, all the sugar that had sunk into their wrinkles luring me. Once they were gone, I'd be left with the mushy, room temperature bran and that was when the battle commenced.

For the most part, I was an obedient kid. On Raisin Bran mornings, my mom would say I couldn't leave the table until I'd had five bites of bran. Once my two scoops of raisins were effectively removed from every bowl—and believe me "two scoops" is quite a generous estimate—I'd cry huge salty tears into my bowl of raisinless sludge. Eventually I'd get my mom to come down to a more reasonable number of bites. Like two. Two massively disgusting, warm bites of chewy brown milk.

I don't eat Raisin Bran anymore. Milk's also out. But raisins I'm still neutral on. The thing with raisins is that they should be added to a food only if they are going to improve its status. Bran flakes? Upgrade. Celery with peanut butter? Upgrade. Cinnamon bagels? That's a close one. Oatmeal cookies? Downgrade.

Now if only I could have talked my mom into putting chocolate chips in my bran flakes. Two scoops, please.

Desserts

INGREDIENTS

1 tablespoon ground flaxseed

3 tablespoons water

1½ cups oats

1 cup whole wheat pastry flour

½ teaspoon baking powder

½ teaspoon baking soda

½ teaspoon salt

½ cup vegan margarine (i.e., Earth Balance) or coconut oil

¾ cup light brown sugar

2 tablespoons organic sugar

1 teaspoon vanilla extract

¼ cup nondairy milk or organic milk

⅔ cup dark chocolate chips

cooking spray, to grease cookie sheet

DIRECTIONS

1   Preheat oven to 350 degrees F.

2   In a small bowl, combine ground flaxseed and water. Set aside to thicken.

3   In a large bowl, combine oats, flour, baking powder, baking soda and salt.

4   Using an electric handheld mixer or a stand mixer, combine margarine or oil, brown sugar, organic sugar, vanilla and milk.

5   Add sugar mixture and flaxseed mixture to flour mixture and mix until just combined. Fold in chocolate chips.

6   Drop spoonfuls of cookie dough onto a cookie sheet lightly greased with cooking spray, spacing them about an inch apart. The dough will not spread much during baking, so press each spoonful into a flat, round shape. Bake for 12 to 14 minutes, or until golden brown. Cool cookies for 1 minute on cookie sheet and then transfer to a cooling rack. Let cookies cool completely before storing in an airtight container.

NUTRITION INFORMATION PER SERVING: 220 calories, 10 g total fat, 3.5 saturated fat, 0 g trans fat, 0 mg cholesterol, 180 mg sodium, 31 g carbohydrate, 2 g fiber, 18 g sugar, 2 g protein, vitamin A 0%, vitamin C 0%, calcium 2%, iron 4%

Based on 15 cookies.

pea points

You can substitute raisins for the chocolate chips... if you're into that kind of thing.

more peas, thank you

Apple Cider Doughnuts

Makes 1 dozen doughnuts

SOMETIMES I THINK THE GIRLS LIKE IT WHEN THEY GET COLDS.

They get special attention. They get their own personal Kleenex boxes, which they decorate with markers and stickers. They get apple cider. In our house, apple cider really just means warmed-up apple juice with a dash of cinnamon. Or on those occasions when Gigi gets to add the spice herself, warmed-up apple juice with an absurd amount of cinnamon, rendering the beverage totally undrinkable.

So with all this apple cider lying around, it was only natural I took the next step. You know, in the name of curing the common cold. Thus, apple cider doughnuts have become a hit in our house, and in the houses of *Peas and Thank You Blog* readers like Kate, who says, "My husband very occasionally will bring home doughnuts for the kids on a special weekend morning, and the kids said these warm doughnuts are better than any doughnut he's ever brought home. Unbelievable."

Oh, I believe it. And I have two kiddos with fake sniffles who believe it too.

INGREDIENTS

1½ cups whole wheat pastry flour

½ cup unbleached all-purpose flour

1 tablespoon baking powder

½ teaspoon nutmeg

½ teaspoon cinnamon

¼ teaspoon salt

¾ cup apple cider

¼ cup organic sugar

¼ cup light brown sugar

2 tablespoons molasses

2 tablespoons unsweetened applesauce

2 tablespoons vegan margarine (i.e., Earth Balance) or coconut oil, melted

½ teaspoon vanilla extract

cooking spray, to grease pan

cinnamon and sugar for dusting (optional)

DIRECTIONS

1 Preheat oven to 350 degrees F.

2 In a large bowl, combine flours, baking powder, nutmeg, cinnamon and salt.

3 In a medium bowl, mix together apple cider, sugars, molasses, applesauce, melted margarine or coconut oil and vanilla extract.

4 Add cider mixture to flour mixture and stir until just combined.

5 Spoon batter into a doughnut pan lightly greased with cooking spray.

6 Bake for 11 to 13 minutes, or until doughnuts are slightly brown and firm.

7 Remove doughnuts from the pan and dust with cinnamon and sugar while still warm, if desired.

NUTRITION INFORMATION PER SERVING: 140 calories, 2 g total fat, 0.5 g saturated fat, 0 g trans fat, 0 mg cholesterol, 140 mg sodium, 29 g carbohydrate, 2 g fiber, 12 g sugar, 2 g protein, vitamin A 0%, vitamin C 0%, calcium 2%, iron 2%

Optional ingredients not included in analysis.

pea points

Since these dough-nuts are not fried, there will be no grease for the cinnamon and sugar to adhere to. If you want the cinnamon and sugar to stick heavily, consider brushing the doughnuts with a bit of melted margarine or coconut oil. But the doughnuts have enough flavor and sweetness with just a light dusting of sugar and spice.

211

Desserts

S'mores Bread Pudding

Serves 8

THERE'S A BAKERY RIGHT BY OUR CHURCH THAT IS MY NEMESIS.

Every Sunday after services, without fail, the car will drive itself to the bakery. It doesn't matter if I've baked blueberry muffins for breakfast and there's a batch of pumpkin bars in the fridge, chocolate chip cookies in the cookie jar and the promise of something new tomorrow. We're at that bakery like clockwork every Sunday at 11:15 a.m. Please don't stalk me.

If there's anything Pea Daddy likes, it's fantasy football. But if there's anything else he likes, it's a deal. I've seen that man try to talk cashiers into taking expired coupons like they'd be signing off on a kidney transplant if they'd just give him the 10 percent off his dress shirt. And this bakery, you see, gives out free slices. I never felt good about this. Sure, free samples get you in the door, but nothing screams tacky like shoving a hot slice of bread in your face and walking right out. Except shoving slices in your kids' faces, too, and walking right out.

It took only about two years of me hiding in the car for Pea Daddy to realize that if he wanted me to accompany him into the bakery and support our weekly pit stop in general, he needed to buy something. It took only one afternoon of the silent treatment for Pea Daddy to realize that if he wanted me to ever bake anything again, he shouldn't buy something that we already had sitting waiting for him at home. It happened with muffins. With pumpkin bars. With chocolate chip cookies.

Enter bread pudding. Besides my eighty-three-year-old grandmother, I know of no one other than Pea Daddy who loves a dessert made out of old bread so much. Especially not the girls. I rarely make it as a result, and so after the bakery by our church started making it, I always encouraged Pea Daddy to buy a piece so we could guiltlessly munch our slices of complimentary multigrain and I could use our bread at home for what it was made for—fresh, fluffy sandwiches.

Desserts

But then came S'mores Bread Pudding. Pea Daddy raved about the version from our bakery so much, I took it as a challenge. And now Pea Daddy has to find something else he can buy when we go each week to the bakery. I think he'll forgive me.

INGREDIENTS

cooking spray or oil, to grease baking dish

5 cups stale whole-wheat bread, cut into ½-inch cubes

6 sheets graham crackers, broken into bite-size pieces

1 cup gelatin-free marshmallows (i.e., Dandies)

1 cup semisweet chocolate chips

½ cup organic sugar

½ teaspoon vanilla extract

½ teaspoon cinnamon

½ cup silken tofu

2½ cups nondairy milk or organic milk

nondairy or organic whipped topping or ice cream, to garnish (optional)

DIRECTIONS

1   Preheat oven to 350 degrees F. Lightly grease a 9 x 13-inch baking dish with cooking spray or oil and set aside.

2   In a large bowl combine bread, graham crackers, marshmallows and chocolate chips.

3   In a blender or food processor, combine sugar, vanilla, cinnamon, tofu and milk. Blend until smooth.

4   Pour milk mixture over bread mixture and stir. Allow mixture to sit for 10 minutes to absorb liquid. Transfer mixture to the prepared baking dish and bake for 40 to 45 minutes, or until bread pudding is firm and just starting to brown.

5   Serve with whipped topping or ice cream, if desired.

NUTRITION INFORMATION PER SERVING: 360 calories, 12 g total fat, 7 g saturated fat, 0 g trans fat, 10 mg cholesterol, 220 mg sodium, 55 g carbohydrate, 3 g fiber, 40 g sugar, 8 g protein, vitamin A 4%, vitamin C 0%, calcium 10%, iron 10%

Optional ingredients and toppings not included in analysis.

Apple Crisp

Makes 8 servings of 1 cup each

MY GIRLS ALWAYS WANT TO HELP ME IN THE KITCHEN.

As a loving, hands-on mom, I'm happy to have their help. Falser words have almost never been spoken. Before you think me unkind, have I mentioned how small our kitchen is? The beauty of it is I can reach our cupboards, our stove and our sink all at the same time. The ugly part is there are my two big feet, two little bodies and at least two step stools in there at the same time. It's like playing Twister with a knife and fire while a battle is being waged over who gets to lick the beater.

Another difficulty is that baking—if you haven't come to this realization yourself yet—is hard. Measurements must be exact. Recipes must be followed. And the one thing that any decent cookie, cake, brownie or muffin recipe will tell you is "Don't overmix." "Don't overmix" means nothing to my children. In fact, when the girls are in the kitchen, mixing becomes a competition, and if one child got to stir the already tough batter one more time, well, the other one has to, too. So no matter what you may assume, you really may want to think twice before eating a baked good from my house. Or at least make sure your jaw is nice and loose, because you may have to do a lot of chewing.

Apple crisp is a lovely solution to all my group baking woes. As is all-day school. While Gigi is in class, I have only one step stool in my way. And when it comes to the somewhat tedious task of peeling and slicing apples, I'm happy to have an extra set of hands. Though Lulu isn't whittling and coring these days, she's a pro at tossing the sliced apples into the bowl. Except for the several slices that inevitably wind up on the floor. Sometimes they get rinsed and put in the bowl. More often they get eaten before I can stop her. Believe me, there's nothing more cringe inducing than watching your child send a cat hair- and coffee ground-covered slice of apple toward her mouth. Perhaps I should do more cleaning and less baking.

But with apple crisp, you can't overmix the apples. The topping is rather forgiving—if you add a few extra oats or a little less cinnamon, you'll still have an amazing dessert. Lulu even had a special hand in this version, a hand, I assure you, that was carefully washed before helping.

As I got out the canister of oats for the topping, Lulu suddenly shouted, "I don't like oat seeds." And thus the oat flour version was born. The topping is a little more delicate, a little lighter and, in my opinion and Lulu's too, a little more delicious.

It's the greatest thing that has ever happened when I've had help in the kitchen. This wonderful development, along with the realization that Lulu will be in school next year, made me rethink my whole approach to group baking.

Grab your step stools, girls. There's always plenty of room for you in here.

INGREDIENTS

cooking spray, to grease baking dish

6 medium tart apples (i.e., Granny Smith), cored, peeled and thinly sliced

2 teaspoons cinnamon

1 tablespoon lemon juice

2 tablespoons light brown sugar plus ⅔ cup

¾ cup old-fashioned oats

½ cup unbleached all-purpose flour

¼ cup vegan margarine (i.e., Earth Balance) or coconut oil

pinch of salt

nondairy ice cream or organic dairy ice cream or whipped topping, to garnish (optional)

DIRECTIONS

1   Preheat oven to 400 degrees F. Lightly grease a 9 x 13-inch baking dish with cooking spray and set aside.

2   In a large bowl, combine apples, 1 teaspoon of the cinnamon, lemon juice and 2 tablespoons of the brown sugar. Toss to coat apples evenly.

3   In a food processor or high-speed blender, finely grind oats. Add flour, margarine or coconut oil and salt, a little at a time, and process until margarine or coconut oil is incorporated and mixture is crumbly.

4   Spread apples in the bottom of the baking dish and sprinkle oat mixture over the top.

5   Bake for 35 to 40 minutes, or until the apples are tender and the top has browned. Serve with nondairy or organic dairy ice cream or whipped topping, if desired.

NUTRITION INFORMATION PER SERVING: 210 calories, 6 g total fat, 1.5 g saturated fat, 0 g trans fat, 0 mg cholesterol, 75 mg sodium, 39 g carbohydrate, 2 g fiber, 31 g sugar, 1 g protein, vitamin A 0%, vitamin C 8%, calcium 4%, iron 6%

Optional ingredients and toppings not included in analysis.

pea points

You aren't limited to apples with this recipe. Use fresh berries, rhubarb and/or peaches in the summer for a delicious, light dessert.

Desserts

Gingerbread Cupcakes with Lemon Cheesecake Frosting

Makes 1 dozen cupcakes

I HAVE A BONE TO PICK WITH THE BREAKFAST POLICE.

It seems some sweet, decadent foods are perfectly fine to eat for breakfast, and others are simply getting the shaft. Muffins sort of toe the line between dessert and breakfast, but no one even bats an eyelash. Cinnamon rolls are totally legit. Pancakes, in their puddles of maple syrup, are respectable. Coffee cake isn't even trying to hide who it is, but it's totally allowed. It has *cake* right in the name, and most of the time, in addition to its brown sugar crumble, it has frosting on it.

So why, pray tell, can we not have cupcakes for breakfast? Do you think the breakfast police might let it slide if it were, say, Christmas? And if we weren't really having just cupcakes, but gingerbread instead? It's not cake. It's bread. And maybe we put just an itsy-bitsy schmear of frosting on top. It has lemon in it. Lemon's a fruit. If it were up to me, you could eat these cupcakes any old time you'd like, Christmas or not.

Even for breakfast.

INGREDIENTS

¾ cup nondairy milk or organic milk

1 teaspoon lemon juice

1 cup whole wheat pastry flour

1 cup unbleached all-purpose flour

1 tablespoon ground ginger

1 teaspoon cinnamon

½ teaspoon nutmeg

1 teaspoon baking soda

½ teaspoon baking powder

½ teaspoon salt

½ cup vegan margarine (i.e., Earth Balance) or coconut oil, melted

½ cup unsweetened applesauce

¾ cup light brown sugar

1 teaspoon vanilla extract

12 paper baking cups or cooking spray to grease cupcake pan

Frosting:

3 tablespoons vegan margarine
(i.e., Earth Balance)

4 ounces nondairy cream cheese
(i.e., Tofutti Better Than Cream
Cheese) or organic cream cheese

2 cups organic powdered sugar

1 tablespoon lemon juice

zest of 1 lemon

DIRECTIONS

1 Preheat oven to 350 degrees F.

2 In a medium bowl, combine milk and lemon juice, essentially
   curdling the milk. Set aside for a few minutes.

3 In a large bowl, combine flours, ginger, cinnamon, nutmeg, baking
   soda, baking powder and salt.

4 Add melted margarine or coconut oil, applesauce, brown sugar and
   vanilla to milk and lemon juice mixture. Stir well.

5 Pour liquid ingredients into the flour mixture and stir until
   just combined.

6 Divide batter among 12 wells of a cupcake pan that has been
   greased or lined with paper baking cups.

7 Bake for 20 to 22 minutes, or until a toothpick inserted in the
   middle of a cupcake comes out clean.

8 Allow the cupcakes to cool completely.

9 To prepare the frosting, whip together margarine, cream cheese,
   powdered sugar and lemon juice. Fold in half of the lemon zest.

10 Frost cooled cupcakes and garnish with remaining lemon zest.

NUTRITION INFORMATION PER SERVING: 330 calories, 13 g total fat, 3.5 saturated fat,
0 g trans fat, 0 mg cholesterol, 330 mg sodium, 52 g carbohydrate, 2 g fiber, 32 g sugar,
3 g protein, vitamin A 0%, vitamin C 2%, calcium 4%, iron 4%

more peas, thank you

Root Beer Cupcakes

Makes 12 cupcakes

PEA DADDY IS A LOYAL MAN.

He's just as into *Star Wars,* vanilla ice cream, baseball cards and Disneyland as he was when he was four. Luckily, he doesn't have the same haircut. This loyalty bodes well for me, though. No matter how nerdy, plain, outdated or juvenile I can be, he's going to love me forever. Fingers crossed.

I tend to be a bit less stagnant. Just because I like something one week—ahem, yoga, juicing and self-taught guitar—that's no guarantee I'm going to like it the next week. I've got a double cushioned mat, a dusty Juice Fountain Plus and a sweet six-string in my garage to prove it.

I guess I'm partially to blame for Pea Daddy's root beer addiction. When I was pregnant with Gigi, I had a big root beer float from a chilled frosty mug every night. I guess *that's* partially to blame for my seventy-pound weight gain. I enjoyed each and every delicious pound. And then I retired the root beer.

But not Pea Daddy. I cannot tell you the lengths we have gone to for a new kind of root beer, a special root beer on tap, an organic keg of root beer. I *can* tell you that Pea Daddy left some clothing behind on our recent trip to Maui so he could stuff his suitcase full of Hawaiian root beer. Luckily, he could spare a bottle of his sweet nectar for these cupcakes. And a new addiction was born.

Desserts

INGREDIENTS

1 cup unbleached all-purpose flour

¾ cup whole wheat pastry flour

1 teaspoon baking powder

½ teaspoon baking soda

1 teaspoon salt

1 cup root beer

⅓ cup maple syrup or agave

⅓ cup vegan margarine (i.e., Earth Balance) or coconut oil, melted

¼ cup unsweetened applesauce

2 teaspoons root beer extract

1 teaspoon vanilla extract

12 paper baking cups, to line cupcake pan

Frosting:
½ cup vegan margarine

2 cups powdered sugar

pinch of salt

½ teaspoon root beer extract

1 tablespoon nondairy milk or organic milk

organic chocolate syrup (optional)

DIRECTIONS

1 Preheat oven to 325 degrees F. Line a 12-well cupcake pan with paper baking cups.

2 To prepare the cupcakes, in a large bowl, combine flours, baking powder, baking soda and salt.

3 In a medium bowl, combine root beer, maple syrup or agave, melted margarine or coconut oil, applesauce, root beer extract and vanilla extract and mix well.

4 Add liquid ingredients to flour mixture and stir until just combined.

5 Spoon batter into the lined cupcake pan and bake 18 to 23 minutes, or until cupcakes are golden and have set.

6 Allow cupcakes to cool in the pan.

7 For the frosting, using a handheld mixer, combine margarine, powdered sugar, salt and root beer extract and mix well. Add milk to reach the desired consistency.

8 When cupcakes are cool, frost generously. Drizzle with chocolate syrup, if desired.

pea points

To make an even lighter version of these cupcakes, use stevia-sweetened root beer, such as Virgil's Diet Root Beer or Zevia Ginger Root Beer.

more peas, thank you

NUTRITION INFORMATION PER SERVING: 280 calories, 12 g total fat, 3.5 g saturated fat, 0 g trans fat, 0 mg cholesterol, 380 mg sodium, 39 g carbohydrate, 1 g fiber, 25 g sugar, 2 g protein, vitamin A 0%, vitamin C 2%, calcium 0%, iron 2%

Optional ingredients not included in analysis.

Peach Cobbler

Makes 8 servings

MY GRANDPA GREW UP IN THE DEEP SOUTH, AND SO BY DEFAULT, I TEND TO CONSIDER MYSELF A SOUTHERNER.

I'm sure this is nothing short of a deep insult to anyone who has ever lived in, visited or even read about the South. But I'm still going to claim some Southern blood every chance I get. It at least allows me to add some twang to my rare, but self-proclaimed "fabulous" karaoke performances. Yeehaw.

I learned a lot of things from my Southern grandpa—how to bait a hook, the simple deliciousness of a perfectly cooked pot of beans, a deep appreciation for country music, corn bread and catching crawdads. He made a mean batch of biscuits, which, I soon learned, also meant he could make a mean cobbler. And though his cooking style was far more Paula Deen than Mama Pea, I can't help but think that somewhere, he's smiling down when I pull a batch of stellar cobbler out of the oven in my old cowboy boots, Hank Williams blaring in the background and a little twang in my voice as I sing along.

Yeehaw.

INGREDIENTS

6 cups peaches, peeled and sliced

⅓ cup organic sugar

2 tablespoons cornstarch

1 teaspoon cinnamon

1 teaspoon lemon juice

pinch of salt

nondairy vanilla ice cream or organic dairy vanilla ice cream, to garnish (optional)

Biscuit topping:

1 cup whole wheat pastry flour

⅔ cup unbleached all-purpose flour

3 tablespoons organic sugar

1 tablespoon baking powder

¼ teaspoon salt

⅓ cup vegan margarine (i.e., Earth Balance) or coconut oil

⅔ cup nondairy milk or organic milk

cooking spray or oil, to grease casserole dish

DIRECTIONS

1 Preheat oven to 350 degrees F.

2 In a large bowl, combine peaches, sugar, cornstarch, cinnamon, lemon juice and salt.

3 In another large bowl, combine flours, sugar, baking powder and salt. Cut in vegan margarine or coconut oil until the mixture has the texture of wet sand. Add milk and stir until just combined.

4 Pour peaches into a 9 x 13-inch casserole dish (or several smaller ramekins) that has been lightly greased with cooking spray or oil.

5 Drop biscuit dough atop peaches in large spoonfuls.

6 Bake cobbler for 30 to 35 minutes, or until peaches are bubbly and biscuit topping is golden brown. Serve with nondairy or organic dairy vanilla ice cream, if desired.

pea points

Feel free to use frozen peaches if fresh peaches are unavailable. I'd caution against using canned peaches, though, as they are generally too soft and will make a quite liquidy cobbler.

NUTRITION INFORMATION PER SERVING: 270 calories, 8 g total fat, 2 g saturated fat, 0 g trans fat, 0 mg cholesterol, 280 mg sodium, 47 g carbohydrate, 4 g fiber, 24 g sugar, 4 g protein, vitamin A 8%, vitamin C 15%, calcium 4%, iron 4%

Optional ingredients and toppings not included in analysis.

Better Cake Pops

Makes approximately 30 to 36 cake pops

These are a totally legitimate knockoff of the Starbucks favorite. I'll even put on a green apron and spell your name on your cup wrong to complete the experience.

LET'S JUST SAY I WALKED INTO STARBUCKS ONE DAY.

Better yet, let's just say I never bragged on our blog about how I gave up coffee. (Sometimes I should really keep my mouth shut. Sometimes I just need a real cup of coffee. None of this weak sauce that Pea Daddy brews every morning and pours into his mug at a fifty-fifty soy creamer to weak sauce ratio. Sometimes I need something that would put hair on my chest, or would at least help me find the ambition to get the girls dressed.

Starbucks saw a little Disney princess "loungewear" action that morning. And then we spotted them: cake pops. The decks were stacked against me in that scenario: a guilty, disheveled mom with two deserving children and pretty pink candy-coated cake on a stick. Ever since I heard of cake pops, I have been morally opposed to rolling mashed-up cake and frosting into balls and dipping them in chocolate or candy. But, dang, they are cute.

Someone must have been watching over me that day. The tall coffee was accidently made a grande. A man with a puppy walked in, the perfect distraction from the coveted treats. And the promise to make our own cake pops at home was enough to get me out of Starbucks alive. With a few heart palpitations and a lofty mission, but alive and cake-pop free.

Mission accomplished.

INGREDIENTS

Cake:

1 cup whole wheat pastry flour

½ cup unbleached all-purpose flour

¼ cup cocoa powder

½ cup organic sugar

1 teaspoon baking soda

1½ teaspoons baking powder

½ teaspoon salt

1 cup water

½ cup unsweetened applesauce

1 tablespoon apple cider vinegar

1 teaspoon vanilla extract

cooking spray or oil, to grease pan

Frosting:

½ cup vegan margarine (i.e., Earth Balance)

2 tablespoons coconut flour or cornstarch

1½ cups organic powdered sugar

1 teaspoon vanilla extract

Coating:

1½ cups semisweet chocolate chips

1½ tablespoons coconut oil

sprinkles, to garnish (optional)

Styrofoam disk, to dry coating

DIRECTIONS

1 Preheat oven to 350 degrees F.

2 In a large bowl, combine flours, cocoa powder, sugar, baking soda, baking powder, salt, water, applesauce, vinegar and vanilla.

3 Spread batter into an 8 x 8-inch pan that has been lightly greased with cooking spray or oil. Bake for 25 to 30 minutes, or until firm. Allow cake to cool completely.

4 To prepare the frosting, beat together margarine, coconut flour or cornstarch, powdered sugar and vanilla. The frosting may seem a bit dry, but resist the urge to add liquid, and just keep beating.

5 When the cake is done cooling, crumble it into small pieces in a large bowl. Add the frosting to the bowl and mix completely into the cake. When the frosting is completely incorporated into the cake, roll mixture into balls that are 1½ to 2 inches in diameter. Set them on baking pans lined with waxed paper. Transfer cake balls to the freezer and let them harden for about 30 minutes.

6 To prepare coating, place chocolate chips and coconut oil in a medium microwave-safe bowl or a double boiler. Melt chocolate completely over medium heat or by microwaving, stirring every 40 seconds.

7 Remove cake balls from freezer, and one at a time, insert a stick into the bottom, dip in melted chocolate and decorate with sprinkles, if using.

8 Place cake pops, stick end first, in a Styrofoam disk. Transfer them to the refrigerator to set up. The coating will harden in as little as 10 to 15 minutes and then the cake pops can be packaged in cellophane or arranged in a cake pop bouquet.

NUTRITION INFORMATION PER SERVING: 120 calories, 6 g total fat, 3 g saturated fat, 0 g trans fat, <5 mg cholesterol, 95 mg sodium, 18 g carbohydrate, <1 g fiber, 13 g sugar, <1 g protein, vitamin A 0%, vitamin C 0%, calcium 0%, iron 0%

Based on 36 cake pops. Optional ingredients and toppings not included in analysis.

more peas, thank you

Blueberry Doughnuts

Makes 1 dozen doughnuts

EVERY ONCE IN A WHILE, I JUST GET LUCKY.

On those rare days, I don't see anyone I know when I'm frantically dropping Gigi off at school in my ratty old bathrobe, with yesterday's mascara smeared all over my face and my hair looking like I got in a fight with a comb, a can of hair spray and a tropical storm. Lord, I miss the eighties.

Every once in a while, Lulu asks for oatmeal instead of Cocoa Puffs in a crowded grocery store. Not often. Every once in a while, I throw a healthy baked good together on a whim, plop it into a doughnut pan for crowd appeal, my aunt stops by to visit and I have fresh blueberry doughnuts to offer her. And then she declares those whimsical doughnuts her favorite ever.

I need that kind of luck more often. Or at least a good face scrubbing and a comb out. Every once in a while.

INGREDIENTS

cooking spray or oil, to grease pan

1½ cups whole wheat pastry flour

½ cup unbleached all-purpose flour

1 tablespoon baking powder

1 teaspoon nutmeg

¼ teaspoon salt

½ cup organic apple juice

¼ cup organic sugar

¼ cup light brown sugar

½ cup unsweetened applesauce

½ cup organic blueberries

½ teaspoon vanilla extract

2 tablespoons vegan margarine (i.e., Earth Balance) or coconut oil, melted

Frosting:
½ cup organic white baking chips

1 tablespoon coconut oil

DIRECTIONS

1 Preheat oven to 350 degrees F. Lightly grease a doughnut pan with cooking spray or oil and set aside.

2 In a large bowl, combine flours, baking powder, nutmeg and salt.

3 In a blender, puree apple juice, sugars, applesauce, blueberries and vanilla.

4 Add blueberry mixture to flour mixture and pour in melted margarine or coconut oil. Stir until just moistened. Spoon or pipe batter into doughnut pan.

5 Bake for 12 to 14 minutes, or until doughnuts are firm and light brown. Allow doughnuts to cool in pan for a minute before transferring them to a cooling rack.

6 Melt white baking chips with coconut oil over a double boiler or in a small bowl in the microwave.

7 Dip doughnuts in melted white chocolate and return to cooling rack to allow frosting to set before serving.

NUTRITION INFORMATION PER SERVING: 190 calories, 6 g total fat, 3 g saturated fat, 0 g trans fat, 0 mg cholesterol, 70 mg sodium, 33 g carbohydrate, 2 g fiber, 17 g sugar, 2 g protein, vitamin A 0%, vitamin C 6%, calcium 0%, iron 2%

pea points

Nondairy white baking chips can be hard to come by. You can find them online or in some natural foods stores. Otherwise, these doughnuts are quite delicious on their own or with a semisweet chocolate topping.

Banana Pudding with Vanilla Wafers

Makes 6 servings of approximately 1 cup each

THOUGH TIMES HAVE CHANGED BOTH WITH OUR TECHNOLOGY AND LIFESTYLE CHOICES, I TRY HARD TO GIVE MY CHILDREN MANY OF THE SAME FOND MEMORIES THAT I HAVE OF GROWING UP.

We build forts in the living room with couch cushions, blankets and giggles. We tape playing cards to the spokes of their bicycles to create that satisfying flapping sound as their wheels spin around our cul-de-sac. We have lemonade stands, even if the only customers are the entrepreneurs themselves. We layer up dishes with banana pudding, banana slices, cookie crumbles and whipped cream. It tastes like heaven. It tastes like childhood. It tastes like a memory in a parfait dish. And it's delicious.

INGREDIENTS

Pudding:

⅓ cup organic sugar

2 tablespoons cornstarch

pinch of salt

1½ cups nondairy milk or organic milk

4 medium bananas, 2 mashed and 2 sliced

2 teaspoons vanilla extract

2 teaspoons lemon juice

¼ teaspoon turmeric (optional)

nondairy organic whipped topping or organic whipped cream, to garnish (optional)

Vanilla wafers:

¼ cup vegan margarine (i.e., Earth Balance)

¼ cup organic sugar

2 tablespoons organic light brown sugar

1 tablespoon nondairy milk

½ teaspoon vanilla extract or vanilla bean paste

¾ cup unbleached all-purpose flour

¼ teaspoon salt

½ teaspoon baking powder

DIRECTIONS

1 To prepare pudding, whisk together sugar, cornstarch and salt in a medium pot. Add milk and whisk until completely smooth.

2 Place pot over medium heat and bring to a low boil, whisking as mixture heats and thickens. Add mashed bananas and cook for an additional minute. Remove from the heat and stir in vanilla, lemon juice and turmeric, if using. Allow mixture to cool before refrigerating.

3 To prepare vanilla wafers, preheat oven to 375 degrees F.

4 Using an electric handheld mixer or a stand mixer, cream together margarine, sugars, milk and vanilla.

5 In a small bowl, combine flour, salt and baking powder. Gradually add flour mixture to sugar mixture, beating until a dough forms.

6 Scoop dough out using a teaspoon and place an inch apart on an ungreased cookie sheet. Press each into a disk.

7 Bake cookies for 7 to 10 minutes, or until the edges start to crisp. Allow cookies to rest on cookie sheet for 1 minute before transferring them to a cooling rack.

8 In 6 parfait glasses, layer pudding, sliced bananas and cookies and top with whipped topping or whipped cream, if using.

pea points

The turmeric in this recipe gives the pudding the traditional yellow color of the boxed pudding mixes of my childhood. You can omit it, if desired. This pudding is best eaten immediately as the bananas will discolor the pudding the longer it sits. Immediate consumption shouldn't be a problem, though.

NUTRITION INFORMATION PER SERVING: 410 calories, 8 g total fat, 2.5 g saturated fat, 0 g trans fat, 0 mg cholesterol, 160 mg sodium, 81 g carbohydrate, 2 g fiber, 59 g sugar, 5 g protein, vitamin A 4%, vitamin C 10%, calcium 10%, iron 6%

Based on 6 servings of pudding (of approximately 1 cup each) and 6 mini vanilla wafers each.

JUST THE BANANA PUDDING

NUTRITION INFORMATION PER SERVING: 240 calories, 1 g total fat, 3 g saturated fat, 0 g trans fat, <5 mg cholesterol, 50 mg sodium, 57 g carbohydrate, 2 g fiber, 46 g sugar, 3 g protein, vitamin A 4%, vitamin C 10%, calcium 8%, iron 2%

Based on 6 servings of approximately 1 cup each.

JUST VANILLA WAFERS

NUTRITION INFORMATION PER SERVING: 40 calories, 2 g total fat, 0.5 saturated fat, 0 g trans fat, 0 mg cholesterol, 25 mg sodium, 8 carbohydrate, 0 g fiber, 3 g sugar, 0 g protein, vitamin A 0%, vitamin C 0%, calcium 0%, iron 0%

Based on 24 mini wafers. Optional ingredients and toppings not included in analysis.

more peas, thank you

Chocolate Peppermint Brownie Cake Pops

Makes approximately 20 to 24 cake pops

THERE ALWAYS SEEMS TO BE ONE LAST DESSERT RECIPE THAT I HAVE TO TUCK IN AT THE END.

I've added this one because our readers requested this healthy makeover. Because you need something festive to serve at a holiday party. Because my kids still beg me for cake pops every time I need a latte. Because one cake pop recipe is never enough. It's a labor of love, people. And I hope it never ends.

INGREDIENTS

Brownies:
¾ cup whole wheat pastry flour

⅓ cup cocoa powder

½ cup organic sugar

½ teaspoon baking soda

2 teaspoons baking powder

½ teaspoon salt

½ cup water

¼ cup canola oil or
melted coconut oil

1 teaspoon vanilla extract

cooking spray or oil,
to grease pan

Frosting:
½ cup vegan margarine
(i.e., Earth Balance)

2 tablespoons coconut flour

3 tablespoons cocoa powder

1½ cups organic powdered sugar

1 teaspoon peppermint extract

pinch of salt

Coating:
1½ cups semisweet chocolate
chips

1½ tablespoons coconut oil

crushed candy canes or
peppermint candies, to garnish
(optional)

Styrofoam disk, to dry coating

DIRECTIONS

1   Preheat oven to 350 degrees F.

2   In a large bowl, combine flour, cocoa powder, sugar, baking soda, baking powder, salt, water, oil and vanilla.

3   Spoon batter into an 8 x 8-inch pan that has been lightly greased with cooking spray or oil. Bake brownies for 20 to 25 minutes, or until firm. Allow brownies to cool completely.

4   To prepare the frosting, beat together margarine, coconut flour, cocoa powder, powdered sugar, peppermint extract and salt. The frosting may seem a bit dry, but resist the urge to add liquid, and just keep beating.

5   When the brownies are done cooling, crumble them into small pieces in a large bowl. Add frosting to the bowl and mix completely into the brownies. When the frosting is completely incorporated into the brownies, roll mixture into balls and set them on baking pans lined with waxed paper. Transfer brownie cake balls to the freezer and let them harden for about 30 minutes.

6   To prepare coating, place chocolate chips and coconut oil in a medium microwave-safe bowl or a double boiler. Melt chocolate completely over medium heat or by microwaving, stirring every 40 seconds.

7   Remove brownie cake balls from freezer, and one at a time, insert a stick into the bottom, dip in melted chocolate and sprinkle with crushed candy canes or peppermint candies, if using.

8   Place brownie cake pops, stick end first, into a Styrofoam disk. Transfer them to the refrigerator to set up. The coating will harden in as little as 10 to 15 minutes and then the brownie cake pops can be packaged in cellophane or arranged in a brownie cake pop bouquet.

NUTRITION INFORMATION PER SERVING: 200 calories, 12 g total fat, 7 g saturated fat, 0 g trans fat, <5 mg cholesterol, 170 mg sodium, 24 g carbohydrate, 2 g fiber, 18 g sugar, 2 g protein, vitamin A 0%, vitamin C 0%, calcium 2%, iron 4%

Optional ingredients and toppings not included in analysis.

Desserts

menu planning

JUST BECAUSE YOU'VE DECIDED TO EAT A LITTLE OFF THE BEATEN path doesn't mean you don't want to entertain. Here are some menus I've put together for a variety of events that may pop up on your social calendar or just for a fun theme dinner with your own brood.

You can thank me via invitation. And airplane ticket. See you soon!

Little Pea's Birthday Party

- PB and J Smoothies, p. 11
- Veggie Crudités with Original Mmmm Sauce, p. 84
- Pizza Popcorn, p. 55
- Italian-Style Meatless Meatball Subs, p. 138
- Better Cake Pops, p. 226

Diner Food Done Better

- Chickpea Melts, p. 132
- Home Fries, p. 26 with Ranch Dressing, p. 58
- Root Beer Cupcakes, p. 221

Sunday Brunch

- Maple Apple Spice Coffee Cake, p. 43
- Fresh Fruit Parfaits with Oatmeal Cookie Granola, p. 8
- Time-Saving Tofu Scramble made with Tofu Seasoning Spice Blend, p. 16
- Jicama Grapefruit Salad, p. 108

Dinner for Two

- Sunshine Kale Salad, p. 134
- Zucchini Quinoa Lasagna, p. 147
- Thin Mint Cookies (for minty fresh breath), p. 189

more peas, thank you

For the Big Game

- Chips with Nacho Mmmm Sauce, p. 86 and Almost Chipotle Guacamole, p. 96
- Cowboy Caviar (even if Dallas isn't playing), p. 127
- Sloppy Josephines, p. 175
- Chocolate Peppermint Brownie Cake Pops, p. 235

Holiday Feast

- Superb Spinach Salad, p. 102
- Corn Chowda with Corn Bread Croutons, p. 110
- Balsamic Roasted Brussels Sprouts, p. 52
- Sweet Potato Dream, p. 76
- Cranberry Blueberry Sauce, p. 71
- Tofu Stuffin' Muffins, p. 152
- Old-Fashioned Pumpkin Pie, p. 198

Almost Just Like Mom Used to Make

- Tofu Noodle Soup, p. 118
- Chickpeas and Dumplings, p. 177
- Apple Crisp, p. 215

A Taste of India

- Black Bean Dal, p. 182
- Coconut Rice, p. 73
- Curry Roasted Sweet Potatoes, p. 60
- Cracklin' Cauliflower, p. 97
- Coconut Cream Doughnuts, p. 186

Fiesta Fresh

- Sunrise Smoothies, p. 2
- Almost Chipotle Guacamole, p. 96
- Tortilla Soup, p. 130
- One Pan Roasted Sweet Potato and Black Bean Enchiladas, p. 158

Buff Mother Breakfast (high protein)

- Creamy Power Porridge, p. 35
- Chocolate Peanut Butter Protein Truffles, p. 63
- Tempeh Bacon, p. 14

converting to metrics

volume measurement conversions

U.S.	METRIC
¼ teaspoon	1.25 ml
½ teaspoon	2.5 ml
¾ teaspoon	3.75 ml
1 teaspoon	5 ml
1 tablespoon	15 ml
¼ cup	62.5 ml
½ cup	125 ml
¾ cup	187.5 ml
1 cup	250 ml

weight measurement conversions

U.S.	METRIC
1 ounce	28.4 g
8 ounces	227.5 g
16 ounces (1 pound)	455 g

cooking temperature conversions

CELSIUS/CENTIGRADE

0°C and 100°C are the freezing and boiling points of water, respectively, and are standard to the metric system.

FAHRENHEIT

Fahrenheit established 0°F as the stabilized temperature when equal amounts of ice, water and salt are mixed. Water freezes at 32°F and boils at 212°F on the Fahrenheit scale.

To convert temperatures in Fahrenheit to Celsius, use this formula:

$$C = (F - 32) \times 0.5555$$

So, for example, if you are baking at 350°F and want to know that temperature in Celsius, your calculation would be:

$$C = (350 - 32) \times 0.5555 = 176.65°C$$

index

A

Agave, xvii
Kung Pao Tofu, 143
Root Beer Cupcakes, 222–23

Almond(s)
Almond Raisin Biscotti, 70
Chocolate Cherry Cashew
Bars, 66–67
Nacho Mmmm Sauce, 86–87
Oatmeal Cookie Granola, 10

Almost Chipotle Guacamole, 96

Apples, xxi
Apple Crisp, 217
Easy Apple Oat Cakes, 39
Maple Apple Spice Coffee
Cake, 43–44

Apple Cider Doughnuts, 210–11

Apple juice, 210
Sunrise Smoothies, 4

Applesauce, unsweetened, xix
Apple Cider Doughnuts, 210–
11
Easy Apple Oat Cakes, 39
Maple Apple Spice Coffee
Cake, 43–44
Maple Dijon Tofu Chops, 150–
51

Artichokes
Spinach Artichoke
Calzones, 162–63

Asian Peanut Slaw, 86

Asparagus
Welsh Rarebit, 85

Avocado
Almost Chipotle
Guacamole, 96
Cowboy Caviar with, 128
Jicama Grapefruit Salad,
108–9
as mayo substitute, 133
Nacho Mmmm Salad, 87

B

Bacon, Tempeh, 14–15

Baking staples, xvii

**Balsamic Roasted Brussels
Sprouts**, 54

**Banana Pudding with Vanilla
Wafers**, 232–34

Bars
Chocolate Cherry Cashew
Bars, 66–67
Strawberry Multigrain Cereal
Bars, 7

Basil
Pesto French Bread, 89
Pesto Mmmm Sauce, 88
Pesto Pizza, 89
Pesto Potatoes, 89
Pesto Tofu, 89

Beans, black
Black Bean Dal, 183
Just Like Mom's Meatless
Meat Loaf, 146
Nacho Mmmm Salad, 87
One Pan Roasted Sweet
Potato and Black Bean
Enchiladas, 159–60
Tortilla Soup, 130–31

Beans, canned, xvii
Carib"bean" Pumpkin
Soup, 105–7
Cowboy Caviar, 128
Green and White Bean
Chili, 120–21

Beans, pinto
Carib"bean" Pumpkin
Soup, 105–7
Chickpea Melts (variation), 133
Italian-Style Meatless Meatball
Subs, 140
Mmmm Nachos, 84
Tempeh Tamale Pie, 164–65

Bean sprouts
Salad Rolls, 86

Better Cake Pops, 227–28

Biscuits
Better Bay Biscuits, 93
topping for Peach
Cobbler, 224–25

Black-eyed peas
Black-Eyed Pea Veggie
Burgers, 180–81
Cowboy Caviar, 128
New Year's, eating for luck
on, 127

Blueberries, xxi
Blueberry Doughnuts, 229–31
Cranberry Blueberry
Sauce, 72

Bread Pudding, S'mores, 214

Broccoli, xxi
Welsh Rarebit, 85

Brownies
Chocolate Peppermint
Brownie Cake Pops, 235–37
Fluffernut Brownies, 197

**Brussels Sprouts, Balsamic
Roasted**, 54

Burgers
Black-Eyed Pea Veggie
Burgers, 180–81
Mexican Millet Burgers, 156–57

C

Cabbage
Asian Peanut Slaw, 86

Cake/cupcakes
Better Cake Pops, 227–28
Chocolate Peppermint
Brownie Cake Pops, 235–37
Easy Apple Oat Cakes, 39
Gingerbread Cupcakes
with Lemon Cheesecake
Frosting, 218–20
Maple Apple Spice Coffee
Cake, 43–44
Root Beer Cupcakes, 222–23

241

index

Calzones, Spinach
    Artichoke, 162–63
Carib"bean" Pumpkin
    Soup, 105–7
Carrot
    Asian Peanut Slaw, 86
    Carrot Miso Dressing, 104
    Carrot Orange Pistachio
        Streusel Muffins, 80–81
    Ginger Soy Soup, 114
    Moroccan Chickpea Stew, 117
    Salad Rolls, 86
    Tofu Noodle Soup, 119
Cashews
    Chocolate Cherry Cashew
        Bars, 66–67
    Corn Chowda with Corn
        Bread Croutons, 110–11
Cauliflower
    Cracklin' Cauliflower, 97–99
    Welsh Rarebit, 85
Celery, xxi
    Chickpea Melts, 133
    Tofu Stuffin' Muffins, 154
Cereal
    Creamy Power Porridge, 36
    Oatmeal Cookie Granola, 10
    Strawberry Multigrain Cereal
        Bars, 7
Cheddar cheese
    Better Bay Biscuits, 93
    Cheddar "Bacon" Scones, 34
    Chickpea Melts, 133
    One Pan Roasted Sweet
        Potato and Black Bean
        Enchiladas, 159–60
Cheese (nondairy), xx
    Better Bay Biscuits, 93
    Cheddar "Bacon" Scones, 34
    Chickpea Melts, 133
    Italian-Style Meatless Meatball
        Subs, 140
    Zucchini Quinoa
        Lasagna, 147–48

Cherry
    Cherry Oat Scones, 23
    Chocolate Cherry Cashew
        Bars, 66–67
Chia seeds, xvii
    Easy Apple Oat Cakes, 39
    Lemon Chia Pancakes, 25
Chickpeas
    Chickpea Melts, 133
    Chickpeas and
        Dumplings, 177–79
    Moroccan Chickpea Stew, 117
    Nacho Mmmm Chickpea
        Salad Stuffed Pitas, 87
    Nacho Mmmm Sauce, 86–87
    Nacho Mmmm Pizza, 87
    Peanut Pita Pizzas, 86
    Pesto Mmmm Sauce, 88
    Roasted Chickpea Tacos, 171
    Superb Spinach Salad, 104
Chiles, green
    Tortilla Soup, 130–31
Chiles, red
    Kung Pao Tofu, 143
Chili
    Green and White Bean
        Chili, 120–21
    Salsa Verde as base for, 90–91
Chocolate
    chips, xviii
    Chocolate Cherry Cashew
        Bars, 66–67
    Chocolate Peanut Butter
        Protein Truffles, 64
    Chocolate Peppermint
        Brownie Cake Pops, 235–37
    coating, with peppermint, for
        cake pops, 235–37
    coating for cake pops, 227–28
    Fluffernut Brownies, 197
    Oatmeal Chocolate Chip
        Cookies, 208
    Orange Chocolate Dream
        Pie, 204–6

S'mores Bread Pudding, 214
    Thin Mint Cookies, 190
Cilantro
    Jicama Grapefruit Salad,
        108–9
    Mexican Millet Burgers, 156–57
    Red Lentil Soup, 122–23
    Salsa Verde, 90–91
Cinnamon
    Maple Apple Spice Coffee
        Cake, 43–44
    Oatmeal Cookie Granola, 10
    Pumpkin Cheesecake
        Muffins, 19–20
    Pumpkin Cinnamon Rolls,
        45–46
    Snickerdoodle Cookie Dough
        Balls, 201–3
Cobbler, Peach, 224–25
Coconut
    Coconut Rice, 75
    how to toast, 188
    topping, 188
Coconut milk, xviii
    Carib"bean" Pumpkin
        Soup, 105–7
    Coconut Cream
        Doughnuts, 188
    Coconut Rice, 75
    Peanut Mmmm Sauce, 85
Coconut oil, xviii
Coffee Cake, Maple Apple
    Spice, 43–44
Condiments, xx
Cookies
    Almond Raisin Biscotti, 70
    Oatmeal Chocolate Chip
        Cookies, 208
    Pumpkin Gingersnap Cookie
        Dough Balls, 192–93
    Snickerdoodle Cookie Dough
        Balls, 201–3
    Thin Mint Cookies, 190
    Vanilla Wafers, 232–34

Corn
  Corn Chowda with Corn
    Bread Croutons, 110–11
  Cowboy Caviar, 128
  Tempeh Tamale Pie, 164–65

Corn Bread Croutons, 111

Cornmeal
  Peach Cornmeal Muffins, 31
  Tempeh Tamale Pie, 164–65

Cowboy Caviar, 128

Cracklin' Cauliflower, 97–99

Cranberry Blueberry Sauce, 72

Cream cheese (vegan), xxii
  Lemon Cheesecake
    Frosting, 220
  Pumpkin Cheesecake
    Muffins, 19–20

Creamy Power Porridge, 36

Cucumbers, xxi
  Cucumber Quinoa Salad, 126
  Quinoa Tabouleh, 94

Curry
  Cracklin' Cauliflower, 97–99
  Curry Roasted Sweet
    Potatoes, 60–61

D

Dairy products
  organic, xx–xxi
  substitutions, xxiii

Dal, Black Bean, 183

Dijon mustard
  Chickpea Melts, 133
  Maple Dijon Tofu Chops,
    150–51
  topping for meatless
    meatloaf, 146

Doughnuts
  Apple Cider, 210–11
  Blueberry, 229–31
  Coconut Cream, 188

Dumplings, 177–79

E

Easy Apple Oat Cakes, 39

Edamame
  Superb Spinach Salad, 104

Enchiladas
  One Pan Roasted Sweet
    Potato and Black Bean,
    159–60
  Salsa Verde for, 90–91

F

Fajitas, Portabella
  Mushroom, 174

Flaxseeds, xx
  Chocolate Cherry Cashew
    Bars, 66–67
  Easy Apple Oat Cakes, 39
  "eggs," 154, 156
  Italian-Style Meatless Meatball
    Subs, 140

Flour, gluten-free, xxiii
  adding xanthan gum, xxiii

Fondue, Mmmm, 85

French Bread, Pesto, 89

Fridge and freezer supplies,
  xx–xxii

Frosting
  chocolate peppermint, for
    cake pops, 235–37
  for doughnuts, 229–31
  Lemon Cheesecake, 220
  powdered sugar, for cake
    pops, 227–28
  Root Beer, 222–23

G

Garbanzo beans. See also
  Chickpeas
  Mexican Millet Burgers, 156–57
  Spinach Artichoke
    Calzones, 162–63

Ginger
  Gingerbread Cupcakes
    with Lemon Cheesecake
    Frosting, 218–20
  Ginger Soy Soup, 114
  Pumpkin Gingersnap Cookie
    Dough Balls, 192–93

Gluten
  gluten-free oat flour, how to
    make, 179
  substitutions, xxiii

Grains, whole, xviii

Grapefruit
  Jicama Grapefruit Salad, 108–9

Grapes, xxi

Green Bean Fries, 62

Green onion
  Asian Peanut Slaw, 86
  Ginger Soy Soup, 114
  Kung Pao Tofu, 143

Guacamole, Almost
  Chipotle, 96

H

Home Fries, 28

I

Icing, powdered sugar, 45–46

Italian-Style Meatless Meatball
  Subs, 140

J

Jicama Grapefruit Salad, 108–9

Just Like Mom's Meatless Meat
  Loaf, 146

K

Kale
  Ranch Kale Chips, 51
  Sunshine Kale Salad, 134–35

Kung Pao Tofu, 143

243

index

more peas, thank you

L

Lemon
Lemon Cheesecake
Frosting, 220
Lemon Chia Pancakes, 25

Lentils, xviii
Just Like Mom's Meatless
Meat Loaf, 146
Red Lentil Soup, 122–23
Sloppy Josephines, 176

Lettuce, xxi
Nacho Mmmm Salad, 87

Lime juice
Salsa Verde, 90–91

Liquid smoke, xx
Tempeh Bacon, 14–15

M

Macaroni and cheese
Mac 'n' Chickpeas, 87
Mac 'n' Mmmm, 84

Mango
Sunrise Smoothies, 4

Maple syrup, xviii
glaze, 44
Maple Apple Spice Coffee
Cake, 43–44
Maple Dijon Tofu Chops,
150–51

Margarine (vegan), xxii

Marshmallow
Fluffernut Brownies, 197
S'mores Bread Pudding, 214

Meatballs
Italian-Style Meatless Meatball
Subs, 140
with spaghetti, 140

Meat Loaf, Just Like Mom's
Meatless, 146

Menu planning, 238–39

Metric conversion table, 240

Mexican Millet Burgers, 156–57

Milk (nondairy or organic),
xx–xxi
Banana Pudding with Vanilla
Wafers, 232–34
Creamy Power Porridge, 36
Lemon Chia Pancakes, 25
PB and J Smoothies, 12

Mint
Chocolate Peppermint
Brownie Cake Pops, 235–37
Quinoa Tabouleh, 94
Salad Rolls, 86
Thin Mint Cookies, 190

Miso
Carrot Miso Dressing, 104

Mmmm Sauces
Nacho, 86–87
Nacho Mmmm Meal Ideas, 87
Original, 84
Original Mmmm Meal Ideas,
84–85
Peanut, 85
Peanut Mmmm Meal Ideas, 86
Pesto, 88
Pesto Mmmm Meal Ideas, 89

Moroccan Chickpea Stew, 117

Mozzarella cheese
Italian-Style Meatless Meatball
Subs, 140
Zucchini Quinoa Lasagna,
147–48

Muffins
Carrot Orange Pistachio
Streusel Muffins, 80–81
Peach Cornmeal Muffins, 31
Pineapple Upside-Down
Muffins, 41
Pumpkin Cheesecake Muffins,
19–20
Tofu Stuffin' Muffins, 154

Mushrooms
Ginger Soy Soup, 114
Portabella Mushroom Fajitas,
174

N

Nachos
Mmmm Nachos, 84
Nacho Mmmm Sauce, 86–87

Nectarines, xxi

Nondairy white baking
chips, 231

O

Oat flour, xix
making gluten-free oat
flour, 179

Oats
Apple Crisp, 217
Cherry Oat Scones, 23
Chocolate Peanut Butter
Protein Truffles, 64
Creamy Power Porridge, 36
Easy Apple Oat Cakes, 39
Italian-Style Meatless Meatball
Subs, 140
Just Like Mom's Meatless
Meat Loaf, 146
Oatmeal Chocolate Chip
Cookies, 208
Oatmeal Cookie Granola, 10
PB and J Smoothies, 12
Strawberry Multigrain Cereal
Bars, 7

Old-Fashioned Pumpkin
Pie, 199–200

Olive(s)
Italian-Style Meatless Meatball
Subs, 140
Nacho Mmmm Pizza, 87
Tempeh Tamale Pie, 164–65

One Pan Roasted Sweet
Potato and Black Bean
Enchiladas, 159–60

Onion(s)
Nacho Mmmm Chickpea
Salad Stuffed Pitas, 87
Salsa Verde, 90–91

Orange Chocolate Dream
Pie, 204–6

Orange juice
Carrot Orange Pistachio
Streusel Muffins, 80–81
Sunrise Smoothies, 4

Organic products
dairy products, xx–xxi
dirty dozen (buy organic), xxi

P

Pancakes
Lemon Chia Pancakes, 25
whole wheat pastry flour
for, xix

Parsley
Chickpea Melts, 133
Quinoa Tabouleh, 94
Time-Saving Tofu Scramble
Spice Blend, 16–17

Pasta. *See also Macaroni and
cheese*
Tempeh Stroganoff, 168–69
Tofu Noodle Soup, 119

Peaches, xxi
Peach Cobbler, 224–25
Peach Cornmeal Muffins, 31

Peanut butter (natural), xviii
Chocolate Peanut Butter
Protein Truffles, 64
Fluffernut Brownies, 197
Peanut Mmmm Sauce, 85
PB and J Smoothies, 12

Peanuts
Chocolate Cherry Cashew
Bars, 66–67
Kung Pao Tofu, 143

Peppers, sweet bell, xxi
Asian Peanut Slaw, 86
Cowboy Caviar, 128
Cucumber Quinoa Salad, 126
Kung Pao Tofu, 143
Nacho Mmmm Chickpea
Salad Stuffed Pitas, 87

Peanut Pita Pizzas, 86

Pesto
French Bread, 89
Pizza, 89
Potatoes, 89
Tofu, 89

Pesto Mmmm Sauce, 88
meal ideas, 89

Pie
crust, 199–200, 204–6
Old-Fashioned Pumpkin,
199–200
Orange Chocolate Dream,
204–6

Pineapple
Peanut Pita Pizzas, 86
Pineapple Upside-Down
Muffins, 41
Sunrise Smoothies, 4
topping, 41

Pistachio
Carrot Orange Pistachio
Streusel Muffins, 80–81

Pitas
Nacho Mmmm Chickpea
Salad
Stuffed Pitas, 87
Peanut Pita Pizzas, 86

Pizza
Nacho Mmmm, 87
Peanut Pita, 86

Pizza Popcorn, 57

Popsicles, from Sunrise
Smoothies, 4

Portabella Mushroom
Fajitas, 174

Potatoes, xxi
Black-Eyed Pea Veggie
Burgers, 180–81
Corn Chowda with Corn
Bread Croutons, 110–11
Home Fries, 28
Pesto Potatoes, 89

Produce
dirty dozen (buy organic), xxi
to keep on hand, xxi

Protein powder
Chocolate Peanut Butter
Protein Truffles, 64
Creamy Power Porridge, 36

Pudding, Banana, with Vanilla
Wafers, 232–34

Pumpkin
canned, xvii
Carib"bean" Pumpkin Soup,
105–7

Old-Fashioned Pumpkin
Pie, 199–200
Pumpkin Cheesecake Muffins,
19–20
Pumpkin Cinnamon Rolls,
45–46
Pumpkin Gingersnap Cookie
Dough Balls, 192–93

Pumpkin seeds
Jicama Grapefruit Salad,
108–9

Q

Quinoa
Cucumber Quinoa Salad, 126
Quinoa Tabouleh, 94
Superb Spinach Salad, 104
Zucchini Quinoa Lasagna,
147–48

R

Raisins
Almond Raisin Biscotti, 70
Moroccan Chickpea Stew, 117
Oatmeal Chocolate Chip
Cookies (variation), 208
Oatmeal Cookie Granola, 10
Pumpkin Cinnamon Rolls
(filling), 45–46

Ranch Dressing, 59

index

Ranch Kale Chips, 51

Rice, brown
Kung Pao Tofu, 143

Rice, brown jasmine
Coconut Rice, 75

Rice noodles
Salad Rolls, 86

Roasted Chickpea Tacos, 171

Rolls
Pumpkin Cinnamon Rolls, 45–46
Salad Rolls, 86

Root beer
Root Beer Cupcakes, 222–23
stevia-sweetened brands, 222–23

S

Salad dressing
Carrot Miso Dressing, 104
for Cowboy Caviar, 128
Ranch Dressing, 59
tahini-lemon, 134–35

Salad Rolls, 86

Salads
Cowboy Caviar, in Taco salad, 128
Cucumber Quinoa Salad, 126
Jicama Grapefruit Salad, 108–9
Nacho Mmmm Salad, 87
Nacho Mmmm Chickpea Salad Stuffed Pitas, 87
Sunshine Kale Salad, 134–35
Superb Spinach Salad, 104

Salsa
Green and White Bean Chili, 120–21
Nacho Mmmm Sauce, 86–87
One Pan Roasted Sweet Potato and Black Bean Enchiladas, 159–60
Salsa Verde, 90–91

Sandwiches and wraps. *See also Burgers*
Chickpea Melts, 133
Italian-Style Meatless Meatball Subs, 140
Salad Rolls, 86

Sauces
Cranberry Blueberry, 72
for enchiladas, 159–60
Original Mmmm, 84
Peanut Mmmm, 85
Nacho Mmmm, 86–87
Pesto Mmmm, 88

Scones
Cheddar "Bacon" Scones, 34
Cherry Oat Scones, 23

Sloppy Josephines, 176

Smoothies
PB and J, 12
Sunrise, 4

S'mores Bread Pudding, 214

Snickerdoodle Cookie Dough Balls, 201–3

Soups and stews
Carib"bean" Pumpkin Soup, 105–7
Chickpeas and Dumplings, 177–79
Corn Chowda with Corn Bread Croutons, 110–11
Moroccan Chickpea Stew, 117
Red Lentil Soup, 122–23
Tortilla Soup, 130–31

Spices, xix
Tofu Seasoning Spice Blend, 16–17

Spinach, xxi
Ginger Soy Soup, 114
Spinach Artichoke Calzones, 162–63
Superb Spinach Salad, 104

Strawberries, xxi
PB and J Smoothies, 12
Strawberry Multigrain Cereal Bars, 7
Sunrise Smoothies, 4

Streusel toppings, 43–44, 80–81

Substitutions
for dairy products, xxiii
for sugar, xxiii

Sunshine Kale Salad, 134–35

Superb Spinach Salad, 104

Sweet potatoes
Cowboy Caviar with, for stuffing, 128
Curry Roasted Sweet Potatoes, 60–61
One Pan Roasted Sweet Potato and Black Bean Enchiladas, 159–60
Sweet Potato Dream, 78

T

Tabouleh, Quinoa, 94

Tacos
Cowboy Caviar for, 128
Roasted Chickpea Tacos, 171

Tahini, xix

Tempeh, xxi
Asian Peanut Slaw, 86
Tempeh Stroganoff, 168–69
Tempeh Tamale Pie, 164–65

Tempeh bacon, 14–15
Cheddar "Bacon" Scones, 34

Thin Mint Cookies, 190

Time-Saving Tofu Scramble Spice Blend, 16–17

Tofu, xxi
Asian Peanut Slaw, 86
firm or extra-firm, xxi–xxii
Ginger Soy Soup, 114
how to press, xxii
Kung Pao Tofu, 143

more peas, thank you

Maple Dijon Tofu Chops, 150–51
Orange Chocolate Dream Pie, 204–6
Pesto Tofu, 89
Salad Rolls, 86
Scramble, 16–17
Scramble, with leftover fajitas, 174
silken and soft, xxii
Tofu Noodle Soup, 119
Tofu Seasoning Spice Blend, 16–17
Tofu Stuffin' Muffins, 154

Tomatillos
Salsa Verde, 90–91

Tomatoes
Black Bean Dal, 183
canned, xvii
Chickpea Melts, 133
Green and White Bean Chili, 120–21
Italian-Style Meatless Meatball Subs, 140
Mmmm Nachos, 84
Peanut Mmmm Sauce, 85
Moroccan Chickpea Stew, 117
Nacho Mmmm Salad, 87
One Pan Roasted Sweet Potato and Black Bean Enchiladas, 159–60
Quinoa Tabouleh, 94
Superb Spinach Salad, 104
Tortilla Soup, 130–31

Tomato sauce, canned
One Pan Roasted Sweet Potato and Black Bean Enchiladas, 159–60
Sloppy Josephines, 176
Tempeh Tamale Pie, 164–65
Zucchini Quinoa Lasagna, 147–48

Toppings
biscuit, for Peach Cobbler, 224–25
coconut, 188

for meatless meat loaf, 146
pineapple topping, 41
for porridge, 36
streusel toppings, 43–44, 80–81
for sweet potatoes, 78

Tortillas
Cowboy Caviar with, for taco salad, 128
Mmmm Nachos, 84
One Pan Roasted Sweet Potato and Black Bean Enchiladas, 159–60
Portabella Mushroom Fajitas, 174
Tortilla Soup, 130–31

Turmeric, 234
Time-Saving Tofu Scramble Spice Blend, 16–17

V

Veggie burgers
Black-Eyed Pea Veggie Burgers, 180–181
Mexican Millet Burgers, 156–57

W

Walnuts
Pesto Mmmm Sauce, 88
Pesto Pizza, 89
Sweet Potato Dream topping, 78

Welsh Rarebit, 85

Whole wheat pastry flour, xix

Wonton wrappers
Ginger Soy Soup, 114

Worchestershire sauce (vegan), xxii

X

Xanthan gum, xix, xxiii

Y

Yeast, nutritional, xviii
Nacho Mmmm Sauce, 86–87
Pesto Mmmm Sauce, 88
Pizza Popcorn, 57
Time-Saving Tofu Scramble Spice Blend, 16–17
Tofu Stuffin' Muffins, 154

Z

Zucchini
Moroccan Chickpea Stew, 117
Zucchini Quinoa Lasagna, 147–48

index

about the author

SARAH MATHENY IS A WIFE AND MOTHER, AND A TOTAL WORK-IN-PROGRESS.

A graduate of Linfield College and Willamette University College of Law, Sarah left her life as a family law attorney to raise a family eight years ago, with every intention of returning to a corner office someday.

Once she actually became a stay-at-home mom, though, the plan quickly changed. She started blogging to share the joys, successes and laughs that come from raising a family with an appreciation of God, and appreciation of each other and, of course, an appreciation of veggies. Through anecdotes and recipes, Sarah has built a following of much loved readers around the country.

She published her first book, *Peas and Thank You,* in 2011 and continues to feed her readers their daily recipe and/or glimpse into life with the Peas at peasandthankyou.com.

She's never looked back. And won't stop looking forward.